I SURVIVED DOZIER

The Deadliest Reform School in America

Richard Huntly

Contact the author:
R.HUNTLY@YAHOO.COM
(661) 532-8050

www.richardhuntlty.com
I Survived Dozier
The Deadliest Reform School in America

Cover design by Gureesha Singh
Gurisha11@gmail.com

Blurb cover photo credited to:
Chris@comstock.com

Printed in the United States of America

In Memory of:

Louise Huntley-Johnson

On April 16, 2018, I lost my sister. She was my mother, dad, and best friend. She was all of that to my siblings and me and was very dear to our hearts. She was our rock. May God continue to keep her. She watched over all of us for more than seventy-two years. I will forever love her. I will forever be grateful for having had her as my sister. Thank you, Dad, for charging her with our care and protection.

Arthur Huntley

My older brother departed this life on April 24, 2020, as a result of a sudden illness. He was my friend. We experienced many challenges in our early years, but together we triumphed. My brother and I were enslaved at the Florida School for Boys.

Willie (Deno) Huntley Jr.

My oldest brother and my friend left me in 1992, thirty days after the loss of our baby sister, Linda. Our time together was short, but you were there to watch over me and offer your protection. I always wished to have had more time with you, but God knew best. I love you, Bro.

Linda Lane

My baby sister, whom I loved so dearly, passed away suddenly in 1992. I will always miss her, and she will forever remain in my heart.

"Death is better than slavery."
Harriet Jacobs

"Slavery didn't end in 1865. It just evolved."
Bryan Stevenson

Acknowledgements

The writing of this book would not have been possible without the help and support of those that continue to be an inspiration to me: My children, Sabrina McNeel, Regina Martin, Midsy Lavern (R.I.P. with daddy's love), Richard Huntly II, Desmond Q. Preston, Marquetta Preston-Patterson; Reginald, Marcos, and William Huntly-Daniels, and Anthony L. Huntley, my oldest—love you all.

My friend, Ms. Marie-Suzi Hyacinthe of Orlando, Florida. My brother Derrexs Suluki of Orlando, Florida. Brother Art Rocker, Chairman SCLC., of Pensacola, Florida. Dr. Erin Kimmerle, anthropologist at the University of South Florida, Tampa, Florida. Roger Dean Kiser, author and child advocate. Ms. Donna Shannon of Ark, Virginia, author of Beyond Mis-Education, editor of Dark Days of Horror at Dozier and of this book—thank you. Ms. Mary Johnson and Mrs. Beverly Roby, whenever I call, you're always there, even in my travels—thank you.

Many thanks to Mr. Evans McKinley of Crescent City, Florida, who welcomed us as guests in his home, and to Mr. Ernest Freeman and his wife Mrs. Marian Norris who took time to show us the Jail where all of this started in Crescent City, Florida. Finally, I thank my entire family, all of whom are a constant source of my strength and purpose, my oldest and youngest siblings Lilly and Luvenia to the greatest extent. You are simply the greatest. Love you all.

Foreword

When I wrote the book, "The White House Boys, An American Tragedy," I did my very best to try to expose the horrible abuses that happened to many boys, both Black and White, who were incarcerated at FSB at Marianna. That was a very difficult thing to do when one has experienced severe abuse, Yet I did not have to experience the even more unbelievable abuses suffered by the Black boys held on the north side of the same campus who were looked upon and treated as less than human. How many of these Black boys survived the brutal, bloody beatings along with the degradation and humiliation they suffered is almost a miracle in itself. How anyone could be treated in such a terrible manner as a young child and leave that facility and make a meaningful life for himself and his family is beyond me. However, somehow my friend Richard Huntly was able to find the inner strength to do just that.

I cannot state in written word how much respect I have for each and every one of the men who survived the trials and tribulations of that period in time in Florida's history.

Let there be no doubt that every story of abuse is important, and my brother's abuse shall also become my abuse. For if I do not stand up for him, then my abuses will also become unimportant. The purpose of a story written from the past is to leave a record so that these same horrible abuses will never happen to another child in the future.

Sometimes it is very difficult to forgive the abuses of the past. Still, even more difficult will be trying to forgive the injustices if another child in the future is abused or killed because we stood by and said absolutely nothing.

Roger Dean Kiser, Sr.

Author/Child Advocate
The White House Boys
http://www.thewhitehouseboys.com
The Books and Stories of Roger Dean Kiser
http://thewhitehouseboys.com/Ameri canOphan/ameicanorphan/index.html

Preface

In the 1950s, I was a slave. Most of you who are reading this book will wonder how that could be possible because slavery supposedly ended in 1865, but it's true. In the 1950s, when I was a very young boy, I was a slave on a modern-day slave plantation located in the rural panhandle of Florida. It was called The Florida School for Boys (FSB), also known as The Arthur G. Dozier School for Boys (Dozier). Yes, this was a "slave plantation" that was masqueraded as a reform school for boys. Instead of the State of Florida bearing the cost of operations, I suspect the state's profit was in the millions.

Parents were told their sons would be made into "good citizens;" however, the boys who resided at this so-called school suffered years of severe physical and mental abuse. The young Black boys ranging in age from ten to twenty-one were forced to do manual labor as slaves on the school's farm including the cane field and other crops, the dairy farm, timber fields, the compost yards, and the slaughterhouse, just to name a few of the for-profit operations. The Florida School for Boys (FSB) was also notorious for the horrors of severe floggings, murder, torture, and even rapes.

For more than two years, I was one of the Dozier boys. Most of the outside world, including my mother, had no clue about what was really happening inside this school. Any boy who might dare to tell of the abuse was discouraged by the threat of death. Sadly, many boys did lose their lives and were silenced forever. As a former slave child, I have become one of the voices for those who were permanently silenced so many years ago. Thank God I am living to tell my story, and I am proud to represent all those boys who are no longer here. In January 2014, The University of South Florida, Department of Archeology, exhumed the remains of 55 bodies from unmarked graves on the grounds of FSB (aka The Arthur G. Dozier School for Boys).

My dedicated mission is to spread the word about the injustices we endured. I co-authored **Dark Days of Horror at Dozier: Rapes, Murders, Beatings, and Slavery** with three other survivors of enslavement at Dozier. I am available for speaking engagements at libraries, high schools, colleges, juvenile detention centers, churches, boys' and girls' clubs, and other nonprofit organizations. I believe it is necessary to enlighten others to the horrors of Dozier and to end the years of silence.

Introduction

During the process of writing this memoir, I have made a sincere effort to tell my story with the utmost truth and integrity. I was a detainee at The Florida School for Boys (FSB) aka The Arthur G. Dozier School for Boys (aka Dozier) from May 1957 until December 1959. More than sixty years have passed since I was discharged from this reform school.

It has taken more than three years to write this memoir. Many of the details were difficult and painful to recall, such as the names of some staff members as well as some of the other young men who lived and worked at the school while I was there. I have made every attempt to describe each event to the best of my knowledge. Still, there are periods where facts may be out of place or confused with respect to location on the campus and the chronological order of occurrences. The important thing I hope readers take away from my story is that the specific events actually occurred.

In 2013, I was a co-author in an anthology describing my experiences at Dozier. While exercising my memory and with a great deal of researched documentation, I discovered some minor discrepancies that were corrected in this memoir. I offer my sincere apology for any inconvenience this may have caused.

PART I
LIFE BEFORE DOZIER

CHAPTER 1
My Beginning

*D*r. John Locke (1634-1704), an English philosopher and physician, declared that the brain of an infant is a blank slate waiting to be imprinted on. I believe this to be true. My very first imprints were not memorable, but I was so happy when my memory took hold because I was a contented child. The remainder of my life rested on my earliest imprinted memories and were the foundation of my stability and survival.

Although my father was a significant figure in my early life, I can't remember his image; I do remember my early life with him. I believe if it were possible for me to see him again, I could single him out from a crowd. I know he has imprinted on my life, and all my memories of him are just waiting to be recalled.

I was somewhere between five and six years old during the most memorable period in my life with my father, my older sister Louise, and my baby sister Luvenia. We traveled the roads from state to state, working the different plantations. Daddy was a seasonal migrant worker. He worked for himself and was never consistently on any company's payroll. It seemed like those were the fun days.

I remember one exciting time when we were with our dad; it was the time of the locust. That was the only time I ever saw a locust swarm in all my life. I was very young, but it was a time I will never forget. The day the locusts were in action was a sight for the eyes to see, and it was as frightening as hell. That day was also shocking to Daddy.

That morning, we went to work with Daddy as always. He had his own car, so we never rode the bus with the other workers, and we could leave the field whenever he wanted.

That particular day we were picking peas in a large field working alongside him. My older sister, Louise, was near me, and Luvenia, who was about three years old, had been placed on the ground close to us. The bus driver was also like an overseer and worked us hard that day. We worked at a fast pace for four to five hours, when the bus driver started yelling in a very loud voice, "Y'all need to hurry! The locusts is coming!" He wanted everyone to hurry and put their gathered peas in a "croaker sack" (burlap bag).

I didn't know why we were being pushed so hard. I knew nothing about locusts, but the bus driver continued yelling for the workers to hurry. I thought it was exciting to see grown people rushing and running about. They even accidentally knocked over several croaker sacks, and the peas spilled out. Seeing them hustling to get them picked up and back in those sacks meant a lot because the people were paid by the pound for their work. Daddy also appeared panicky as he pushed and rushed us.

The bus driver appeared terrified, and he started yelling even louder, "Rack-um and sack-um up!" he screamed. "We got to get on the bus! Hurry! Hurry! We got to get on the bus! Sack-um up, y'all! The locusts is coming! Hurry up and put everything in the bag as you go!"

Someone in the crowd yelled out, "Look at the sky! Oh, hell!" People were hustling and running toward the bus. Daddy didn't have time to get us to his car, so we were loaded on the bus along with all of the other people. The three of us shared a seat, and Daddy stood hovering over us. He didn't seem to be as excited by this event as the other people, probably because we were safe, and this wasn't his first time seeing a locust swarm.

We sat in awe and gazed out the window, watching as the insects went to work, quickly devouring all vegetation in their path. The multitude of grasshoppers sounded like a loud harmonic humming noise; you could literally hear the leaves and stalks in the field being eaten. Some of the last people to get on the bus were covered with grasshoppers. Some of the folks were helping them pull the bugs off.

I don't think I will ever forget that day when the sky went dark with locusts. They hummed and buzzed about in a wild and frenzied way. Everything in their path was being attacked—people, plants, and the peas. Suddenly, I understood why the driver was yelling. The locusts didn't try to eat the burlap bags. Everyone kept their eyes on the rows in the field where they had been working. When it was all over, millions of locusts had invaded the fields. In less than two hours, the pea field had been stripped of all greenery. Then the black cloud of locusts swarmed off, most likely in search of another field. Only a few bugs remained behind to continue gleaning the field.

It's amazing that I should remember the "day of the locust" so vividly. The memory pictures of that day are so clear in my mind, but I can't remember my dad's face; that has always worried me.

CHAPTER 2
Gone was the Life I Knew

7he end of those times with Daddy was fast approaching. He was traveling the last mile of his way. I was still very young, six or seven years old. The span between the happy and the sad times is fuzzy. I didn't know the happy times were about to end, and the sad times were about to set in. I didn't know trouble would be in my way for years to come.

Daddy was seriously ill, but being so young, I did not know it. I don't believe he ever complained of feeling ill or being in pain. He was mentally strong and courageous. Later, I learned he had cancer. He was too sick to travel for work, but he took one last road trip. He had one last mission before leaving this earth. He needed to locate our mother. He needed her to care for the three of us after his death. I didn't know if he knew where she was. I do know he found her in a town called Crescent City, Florida.

Mama and Daddy had separated before I reached a time in my life when I would question why. It wasn't until later in life I learned about my parent's separation. I never questioned where Mama was, or if we even had a mother. All I knew was that all who were important to me were Daddy, Louise, and Luvenia, because at the time, I didn't know my other siblings. There were many answers in my life, but I did not have the questions.

For whatever reason, Mama was afraid of Daddy. I was told that when she found out Daddy was in town and he was looking for her, she feared for her life. She gathered my other siblings and moved from her house. While seeking safety from him, she went to her boss-lady, Ms. Jerri, who directed her to the police.

Mama wanted to be sure the police arrested Daddy, so she told them he had an extensive criminal past. This included many assaults against the police, jail, a prison break, attempted murder, and his unpredictable behavior. She told them that he broke a policeman's jaw and made attempts against her life. She also told them that her son, our brother, Willie Jr, was detained at the Florida Industrial School for Boys in Marianna, Florida, for stealing. (The name was changed to The Florida School for Boys when I was there.)

The police eased Mama's mind by informing her of Daddy's arrest due to her allegations. They held him for a period of two or more weeks. During that time, he had severe hemorrhaging and weight loss; they could see he was a very sick man.

The early 1950s was not a period where verification of an accusation was a keystroke away. Daddy, being a Black man, was not given the benefit of offering a defense. The police checked old records, arrest logs and sought to gather information from a neighboring jurisdiction. Daddy told the police the circumstances of his marriage, the children, his terminal illness, and the reason he needed to find his wife. After a couple of weeks, maybe three, and a thorough investigation of Daddy, the police cleared him and set him free.

We were staying with Daddy's girlfriend, Miss Addie, and feared he would not return. I was afraid because of the many days he was away. Later, we discovered what happened; what Mama told the police about him had a lasting effect on me.

Daddy was different when we saw him again. His overall appearance had transformed slowly, so I didn't recognize the change in him. I did recognize the dullness to his darker brown completion, his loss of vibrancy and energy, but older people got tired easier than kids my age.

———— ഇൽ ————

Two police officers visited Mama while she was still in hiding to give her an update on the situation. She was informed that they had nothing to hold Daddy on. Something happened between the two of them that caused her to fear him, but the police assured her he was no longer a threat. They described him as a small thin, brittle man who was frail and weak. They said he told them he was in the last stage of cancer and hemorrhaging. He had also informed the police about all of his children, the ones that lived with him, and the one that still lived with her. He needed to know where the children could be brought upon his death. He had asked them to give her that message. They continued to tell Mama all he wanted was to get back to his children, and later, after his death, which he believed wouldn't be long, he wanted her to take full custody of them.

Daddy was able to return to us without any farther incidents. He had searched and searched for our oldest sister, Lilly Mae, but his time ran out; he couldn't find her. My mother had allowed her to live with her sister, and my aunt placed her in a home for girls. My aunt refused to tell Lily Mae that Daddy was looking for her before he passed.

Daddy gave Miss Addie the particulars of how to have my older brother, Willie Junior, nicknamed Dino, released from FSB. His life was short from that point. His earthly travels ended abruptly; within days, he laid down and took his last breath. Life also seemed to end for me that September in 1954, in a place called Elkton, Florida. That was where our daddy, Mr. Willie Huntley, passed away.

Daddy's girlfriend, Miss Addie, or maybe she was his fourth wife—the details of their relationship were never clear to us—arranged his funeral and burial in Armstrong, Florida, which was one mile north of Elkton, Florida. Sadly, only five of us were there, Miss Addie, my baby sister, Luvenia, Louise, Willie Jr., and me.

After seeing Daddy laying lifeless in that casket, I began to realize he was gone; it didn't register until then. We all watched as he was being rolled out of that church and then laid to rest forever in the damp, dark earth.

It's almost sixty-six years later now, and as I write this, it still seems like yesterday. Daddy's last words to me were, "You're going to have to be the man for Daddy now, okay?" Those words began to shape my life.

ᕮᕭ

Daddy trusted Mrs. Addie to be a guardian for us, but shortly after his death, we were taken to our mother's house in Crescent City, Florida, and left there by ourselves. There was no one home, but we were left on the porch of that little gray wooden house anyway. Mama was still away for fear of Daddy. The neighboring friends rescued us and took us home with them. Mama returned to her home as soon as she received the message. There she found four special delivered packages waiting for her. In addition to my two sisters and me, now there was Deno.

My baby sister, Luvenia, and I didn't remember our mother. Luvenia was still sucking a bottle when our mama and daddy separated. We also had no memories of our brother, Willie Jr. (Deno), until he was returned at Daddy's funeral.

After leaving Daddy for at least five years, Mama had started a new life, and she had a new baby. We had just heard about this, and that was surprising news even to Louise. I wondered if we were delivered to the right place; was this really our mama? For all I knew, my baby sister was with us, and her name was Luvenia.

When Mama arrived, she had our brother Arthur (Art) with her, and my baby sister. I did not remember Art; he was a year older than me. We found out the news about the new baby was true. We officially had a new baby sister. Her name was Linda; she was born in Crescent City, Florida, and she was two years old.

Mama was a real mother; she didn't deny us but took us in with open arms. She did the best she could with the situation at hand. Her responsibility grew from two children to six overnight.

She found out the real truth from my older sister about Daddy and the circumstances of his illness and death. She also found out about what personal property he may have left for his children. She wanted to know how we all arrived at her home. Louise told her that Daddy had a car, and all of his things were at Miss Addie's. She also told Mama where we were staying in Elkton.

Mama made arrangements and took us back to Elkton to collect Daddy's belongings. She tried to get his car and his other things from Miss Addie, but that didn't happen. We returned to Crescent City empty handed. I am sure Daddy would have turned over in his grave knowing we would be stripped of everything—money, car, and whatever else he left to us.

CHAPTER 3
A New Beginning

*I*n the beginning, it was a beautiful experience getting to know all of my family, but it wasn't long before reality began to set in. Mama was working, but her income wasn't enough to support her new family. When Mr. Willie, Mama's dear friend, found out she had other children, I think that ended their relationship. Times got to be very hard for us after that.

୧ଜ

Deno was with us for a while, and then he was gone. I was told Mama allowed him to be adopted by a family who was childless and who promised to give him a good life. I was twelve years old when I met him again. We formed a lasting relationship, never to be penetrated except by death. Deno died while sleeping late in 1996, without warning. I like to think he is with Daddy now.

I didn't know how long my mother and Art were in Crescent City before we arrived, but he was well-known around town. I started hanging out with him. He was very excited to show me around town, at least where his friends hung out at the playground and his buddy's house. He took me around to different places after school and rode me on the handlebars of his bicycle. I didn't think he really knew how to ride with someone else on the handlebars that well, so most of the time, I preferred to walk.

Arthur often asked me if I wanted to go with him to his friend's house. "We could come back home fo' night," he declared. "You wanna go wit' me or go home?"

"Naw! I'm goin' wit'cha to ya friend's house," I answered.

"Com'on den, Richard. We gotta hurry up. You better keep up, 'cause we gotta catch the bus. If somebody sees us and tells Mama, we're gonna get a whippin'. We supposed to be going home, not catching the school bus."

Everything around me was new, not just around town. I had been living in a very well-protected community and had no worldly experience. This was my first time even being away from home, and I felt vulnerable.

Art said the school bus would take us to his friend Robert's house who lived in the country and they had a mule. Art and his friends took turns riding Molly, the mule.

Robert soon asked, "Who is that wit' you, Art?"

"My lil' brother."

"Man, where he been? I ain't never seen him before."

Robert was a dark fellow, and he squinted his eyes as if he didn't like me. I wasn't afraid of him, because I didn't like him the least bit either. I didn't know where that attitude came from, but I was quiet and stayed on the defense. I did not want to answer a lot of his questions.

"What's your name?" he asked in a louder than normal voice.

Art jumped to defend me. "Man . . . I told you, this is my brother, dog! He's alright! Leave him alone; he just moved down here, man!"

Later that evening, just before dark, my brother and I headed toward home. While we were at Robert's, I couldn't leave for home on my own because I didn't know where we were. I was lost. We had to walk because there was no school bus to deliver us back to our neighborhood, and it was a long walk. I was tired and walking as fast as I could. Art could walk faster than me. He kept yelling, "C'mon, Richard!" He walked the hell out of me because he was trying to get back home before night fell.

Mama was probably going to kill us anyway because she didn't know where we had been for so long. Aside from our fears about Mama, I had no idea what else could happen. I was with my big brother. I felt safe. I wasn't worried about anything else going wrong, even though we were already in enough trouble. However, the later it got, the more afraid I became, and all the while, I was sure we were close to home. I was like a sheep being led to slaughter.

A policeman saw us walking, or maybe someone called him, we never found out what happened. This policeman was known by his nickname, "White Cap." He drove up to us, stopped, got out of the car, and asked, "What y'all doing out here?"

Art began telling White Cap where we were coming from, where we lived, and how we were in trouble because we were late. I didn't know all of the words Art was saying. I was so young; I guess that's why White Cap didn't ask me anything. I could not have told him anything anyway.

White Cap ordered us into his car; then, he drove off. I thought he was taking us home, but instead, he took us to jail, I mean a *real* jail. I was only eight years old and scared to death.

White Cap literally threw us in jail, shoving us into the small, one-story building and then into two cells, my brother, Art in one, and me in the other. I don't know why he didn't put both of us in the same cage. It was dark and scary in there. Back then, I called it "that place." I had never seen anything like it before, so I didn't know what to call it until later when I learned it was a jail. When White Cap slammed shut that cage and shook the door to make sure it was locked, Art didn't say anything. I said, "Hey, sir, we gotta stay here?"

"Yeah, boy," he replied. "I'mma teach y'all not to steal nutten from round hea'!"

God knows, I had no idea what he was talking about, I really didn't. My troubles started right there in that little cage-like jail.

Crescent City community jail. In 1954, my brother Arthur and I were held there for two days without our mother's knowledge. The police said we were "looking for something to steal." We were lost passing through the white folk neighborhood trying to get home; the police White-Cap, put us in jail for doing so. I was only eight years old at the time. Credited to: Mr.& Mrs. Ernest and Marian Norris Freeman. Of Daytona Beach Fl. 7-5-19

From the glow of a dim light, I saw a flat steel frame with a mattress, sheets and a blanket, the cinderblock walls, and bars on the window. It was obvious, this wasn't good. From the outside, the building looked almost like a regular little house. The hard floor sounded like grit wherever I walked. The jail was empty except for us; whoever was in that cage before me had left food in a plate that was covered with maggots.

The police kept us in there for about two days. Mama had been looking for us all that time. I guess she didn't know anything about a missing person reports if there was such a thing back then. White Cap returned us home and told her that she better do something with us saying, "'cause we don't do no stealin' round hea'!"

Mama yelled at us, "Why the hell the police is bringin' y'all home! What did y'all do?"

White Cap told her he had us in jail cause we were "looking for somethin' to try ta steal." He then left.

Mama turned to us again. Her face showed relief, fear, and anger. "What y'all do?" she asked again.

Defending myself, I answered Mama, saying, "Arthur told me he knew where he was going, and he knew what he was doing. He said, 'just c'mon boy.' I didn't know how to come back by myself, so I stayed with Arthur."

The result of that arrest put my brother and me in the criminal system, and that resulted in long-term misery.

Years later, I found out the charge was "looking for something to steal."

Basically, we spent two days in that place because the police said we were, "try'na steal somethin'," without seeing anything we stole. We were only innocent little boys looking for a way home. The real charge was, we were little Black boys walking in the wrong neighborhood.

Our mother continued to question us, but she decided to take sides with White Cap. She believed whatever the White folk said. They were right because "White people ain't gon' tell ya no lie. Not White people." She believed that with all her heart.

I learned at an early age that not just my mother, but mostly all Black people during that era thought the same way. To satisfy the White man, they did unbelievable things just to catch Black people. Whatever the White man said or did was right or fine with them. I do remember when I was a young boy, the old-timers around us used to say, "Ya do what dem dar White folks tell y'all boy, 'cause dey ain't gonna neva tell ya nothin' wrong." Ain't that a blip?

Before I arrived in Crescent City, I was not accustomed to being around so many White people. I began to see these people as they were, *mean*, and it was an awful experience trying to understand them. As a youngster, I wondered where all these people came from and how they got here, because they were not in Elkton. Elkton had been my whole world. It was where my life began to shape and form. We never visited towns or cities where large groups of people resided. Therefore, such an abundance of people of all colors, except for Blacks, were absent in my little world. I learned later in life, the house we lived in and the surrounding houses were not on the so called White plantation farm, but Black people owned their property or rented it. Unlike Elkton, in Crescent City, White people were everywhere. The relationship between the Blacks and Whites, and how the Blacks were subservient to the Whites, was also new to me.

Soon it was time to register for school. I attended school in Elkton, but I guess that was some kind of play center compared to the school system in Crescent City, where I had to be registered in a real public school.

At eight years old, I had never attended a real school before, and it was hard for me to adjust. Although Daddy took us all over the north, my memory was skimpy at best. Elkton was the place I remembered the most, but to live anywhere outside of Elton's lifestyle was living in the fast lane. It would take me a while to catch up.

Slowly, I began to get accustomed to my new surroundings. I did my best, but an occasional incident of speaking out in class didn't help. It really didn't help when I pulled my shirt off while in class because I was hot. I was a young fellow and had not been shaped or molded by the words "fear," "shameful," or "comical."

Part of my problem was a bald head. The boys and men were wearing hi-right and lo-left haircuts in those days. My hair was known as, "the mail man's route." It used to draw up really tight. There wasn't a comb made to do my hair justice, not yet anyway. Imagine, sitting at my school desk sideways with my shirt off, a bald head, talking loud, and yelling out, "Y'all tired? So y'all don't wanna play no mo'? Okay." However, that was soon straightened out by our teacher. Her name was Mrs. Gladys. She thought because I had attended school before, I knew the rules, but I didn't.

In Elkton, Florida, just thirty miles away, children played in school and did what they wanted to do. At the Middleton-Barney School, in Crescent City, when I pulled off my shirt because I was hot, I got in trouble. I wanted to continue playing, but recess time was over and we had to return to class. That didn't sit well with me. I blurted out in class, again, "Why y'all don't want to play no mo'?" Everyone thought that was funny; they just looked at me and laughed. I really didn't understand what the big deal was. I kept asking the question, but my questions went unanswered.

"You don't just blurt out in class," Mrs. Gladys said. She was not laughing, and her tone was stern. I guess I was the class clown without realizing it.

Mama was called out to the school a couple of times, but I didn't think things were that bad. During those visits, she explained to the principal and staff who we were, and what the conditions were like in Elkton before I came there. After those visits, conditions at school were better because I began to understand the rules a little better and didn't blurt out in class like before.

While at the Barney Elementary, Art and I skipped school a time or two. He took me to where fishing boats came in. There were lots of fish in large crates. We were welcome to take a few.

Arthur knew a lot about fishing. There was a lake across the street in front of Mr. Lane's house. His house sat on the corner, facing the lake. We lived right behind his house, which seemed to be Art's favored fishing place. We went to the lake a few times to fish. I didn't like fishing, whereas he did. To me, fishing was a complete waste of time. Even at the age of eight or nine, I didn't like many of the things Art wanted to do. We simply had different interests, but I went along with him because I was green and didn't have a choice.

I believed it would have done me all the good in the world if I could've gone back to Elkton. I was happy there, and life was so much easier for me. I used to feel like I wanted to cry when I thought about how much my life had changed since Daddy died. I missed him, and I wished we didn't have come to this place. Just having someone to play with was difficult. I was too young for Mama to let me go anywhere alone. I wasn't allowed to play at other kid's houses unsupervised. Grown people around us were so nosey, always picking children's minds and questioning them to find out what was going on at their homes. This was another reason Mama made me stay with Art; she didn't want other people picking me for information about our life.

I knew and understood that Daddy wasn't coming back. I realized I would have to adjust and settle into my new life. There were times when I remembered Daddy's words. I assumed he was losing his grip on life because he called to me, saying, "Son, I'm not going to be with y'all much longer. I got to leave y'all, and you're gonna have to be the man for Daddy. Okay?"

"Yes, sir, Daddy," I responded.

When we lived at the house behind Mr. Lane, the welfare people helped us, making sure we had food and clothes, although they were mostly girl's clothing. It was only two of us boys left, Art and me. Deno had been adopted, and Mama applied for Daddy's social security and received it. I'm sure that lessened her struggles. Getting clothes and food for us was her biggest worry. She did the best she could by continuing to work, but it was not enough to fully support us. Eventually, Mama decided to move back to Orlando to start life over again.

CHAPTER 4
Moving Back to Orlando

I started making friends in Crescent City through Art. Now that I was beginning to settle in, it was time to move again. We were moving back to Orlando, where I was born. This new move would prove to be the most challenging move of all.

While in Crescent City, Art and I were continuing to attend the Middleton-Barney School. Mama knew our oldest sister Louise was watching us; after all, that had been her job for God knows how long. With that dependable help, she could move about rather freely to do what was necessary to complete her plan.

Perhaps she was making arrangements for our big move back to Orlando. I thought we were supposed to go to school, but for whatever reason, Mama left us home that day. She was gone for a long time, and we finished doing what she told us to do. Art decided to go to the lake across the street from the house and take me with him since Mama told him to keep up with me. I may have been nine years old by then, or pretty close to it.

At times we were harassed by the police, and we were certainly always watched by the neighbors. It seemed like everywhere we turned, the police were present. My brother Arthur had been in this town for some time, and he never had any trouble with the police. Why now? Maybe the school reported our absence or a nosey neighbor called the police after noticing us at the lake. I looked up, and there was White Cap walking toward us.

I thought, *Why is White Cap always harassing us?* We were ordered into the police car and taken to school. He left word that when he returned to the school, he was going to whip us.

Later that day, White Cap did return to the school. I didn't know what we had done wrong. Mama had not sent us to school that day; she left us at home under our big sister Louise's care because she was preparing to move us back to Orlando. We were supposed to stay home, but Arthur wanted to go across the street to fish, and Mama told me to stick close to Arthur, so when he left the house, I went with him.

It seemed like Art and I just couldn't get it right for one reason or another. We were kept after school and ordered to remain in our classes. Understand, this was a time before school integration; these were my people participating in this incident. When White Cap returned to the school, this time, he had the principal bring my brother and me to his office separately.

This was another experience that will forever be remembered. The Principal spoke to me. I don't remember his words, but deep inside, I believed something wasn't right. I probably would have left the school, but the problem was Art. We were separated, and I couldn't get to him in time so we could leave together. I didn't know I was being led into the principal's office to be whipped. Two or three teachers were in there with White Cap waiting for me. Immediately, I wondered why so many people were in there.

They took me into the office and shut the door. White Cap took his belt off and started stripping his big black belt of all the accessories it was holding—his gun and holster, his handcuffs, and other stuff. While staring me straight in my eyes, he said, "I'm fit'na beat yo' ass, boy."

I only stared at him.

"Yeah, I'm fit'na beat you!" he said again.

"No, you ain't!" I shouted. I don't know where the defiant tone came from, but I yelled it out. I was scared. He had a mean look on his face and a threatening tone in his voice. One of the teachers snatched me around, and I slipped to the floor. Staring up at all of them, I yelled, "Stop holding me! Y'all stop holding me down here!"

One of the Black teachers said, "You don't talk to the police that way." I'm sure my response sent a shock wave through all of the Black teachers at that school. They had never heard a little nigger boy say that to a White man before, especially the police.

White Cap really had a mind to beat the hell out of me that day, especially when I said, "No, you ain't!" as if saying that gave me any hope of changing my fate. It didn't. My Black principal and teachers grabbed me the minute I said that. White Cap himself probably couldn't believe what he heard from a little colored boy. He was as mad as a raging bull, and it showed. I was pulled across a chair, with one of the male teachers holding my legs, and the other two female teachers held my hands.

White Cap started hitting me across my back and legs with his thick belt. I began hollering and yelling out. A White man had never laid a hand on me until then. The thought of Daddy's words entered my mind, "You gonna have to be a man now." "Yes, sir," I said. At that moment, my hollering stopped. I wasn't saying anything. Anger just set in. I began to wiggle violently, trying to snatch myself free. As the police continued to hit me, I was determined not to be outdone, but he really whipped me that day.

They released me and I stumbled to the floor, pulling away from them. I didn't fear this White man anymore, and I was confused by my own Black people holding me down. I didn't understand why they were helping this White man. It is said that "God protects babies and fools." I guess I was both. One of the teachers led me back to my empty classroom, where I waited on Art. I am almost sure Art hadn't ever had a White man lay hands on him either. On the way back to my class, I heard Art hollering, so I assumed the same thing was happening to him.

We told Mama what happened at school; it was useless. She felt helpless because a policeman was the one who did it. She assumed it was something else we did wrong, according to the police. That was almost sixty-six years ago, and Art and I talked about it until shortly before his death this year (2020).

In 2016, I returned to Crescent City, Fl. in search of the school I was attending when I was beaten by White Cap in 1954. I am told this is the original Middleton Burney School. It has been renovated many times since then. A historic section of it remains standing. My sincere thanks to the staff that gave me the information.

Honestly, I didn't know much about White people when traveling with Daddy. We never came into contact with them that much, or at all. I certainly never saw Black and White people interact enough to speak of anyway. When we worked at different places, a Black man was always in charge, so I didn't know I was supposed to be afraid of White people. I believe that was why I didn't have any fear of them.

While traveling with our dad, we met a little White boy and girl in one of the places we worked. We played together and got along. Our acquaintance was short-lived because we moved on. That was all I knew about White people at the time. I had no ideas or understanding of racism or segregation. All of that came later, and I still didn't understand it when I saw it.

෨෨

I'm not sure how long we attended the Middleton-Burney Elementary School after that incident. Mama felt helpless at trying to protect us. She finally got the things she needed, and life in Crescent City was slowly nearing its end. I, for one, can say I was happy, but I didn't realize wherever you go, starting over was another challenge.

Although I was rather young, I still wondered why trouble was always present. I did have more of an attitude than most boys my age. I believe that was because I wasn't raised to be subservient the way slaves were. I wondered if Daddy had moved us to that secluded area in Elkton to keep us out of the hands of the White man.

Finally, we moved from Crescent City back to Orlando, Florida, where we were originally from. However, the wheels of injustice continued to follow us; it was about to start all over again.

Mama registered us at Callahan Elementary School. As a matter of fact, some of my favorite memories are of my time at that school. Mrs. Hawkins was my teacher. She had two theories, which I thought were outstanding.

"First, believe it or not, some of you in this class will be living when the world ends. Second, I would like everyone in the class to stand and state what you want to be when you grow up. Think tank," Mrs. Hawkins would say.

All the kids were saying a doctor, a pilot, police, teacher, etc. When everyone had answered, Mrs. Hawkins stood in the front corner of the classroom and said, "I didn't hear anyone say they wanted to be a mechanic, a garbage man, a truck driver, or the work your mama or daddy does now, but twenty years from now (this was in the early to mid-fifties) you will need a twelfth-grade education just to be a ditch digger."

Her lesson stayed with me until this day. I used to think I was left out of that equation before I found myself. During that class, I believed I had found the key to a good life.

In Orlando, I liked my teacher and my new beginnings in the city where I was born. We were back home now, and life was going pretty well. I didn't remember much about Orlando, but people remembered us on sight. My older sisters remembered a lot of people, too. Everywhere we went, somebody was calling out our name; it wasn't a bad thing at all.

Mama always gave wise counsel to my older brother and sisters about the streets. They were much older me; I was kind of small back then, being the baby boy.

It was strange and wonderful having all of us back together again after such a long separation. Our oldest sister, Lilly Mae, returned home also. She and my next oldest sister, Louise, were both young ladies now. Only Deno was absent.

For a short while, the family was happy being on familiar territory. Although we were back in Orlando, we were moving to another part of town. A change of school was necessary, but not before Mrs. Hawkins passed away in 1956. I was allowed to attend the funeral and say my personal goodbye to her.

By now, I had attended three schools in less than two years. I remember being enrolled at the Holden Street Elementary School, but since I spent so much time in detention, I don't remember much more about the school. At the Callahan School, Mrs. Hawkins was my most loved and most unforgettable teacher; however, I had another love—I will call it "puppy love" for a girl that sat in front of me in class. I used to love to just look at her, and to get her attention, I would pull her long pretty hair. She would stare at me as if she could kill me. I didn't care because I got her attention the only way I knew how. I could've looked at her all day. About thirty years later, we did meet again, and that piqued our interest. Instantly, sparks flew, and thoughts from the past returned to us.

Mama had a difficult time keeping up with Arthur. Whenever she gave him a little room, he would pull a disappearing act; no one could tell which direction he went.

I thought Art was the smartest person alive. I wanted to follow him everywhere he went; however, as time went on, I paid a heavy price that proved detrimental to me in the near future. I didn't know long and hard times were close, but at the time, making new friends and learning to be around other people was nice.

It wasn't long before I made friends of my own with kids from the neighborhood. It wasn't hard to do; riding bikes, shooting marbles, playing stickball, and a few other games, was good. However, it was not all fun in the beginning. Every neighborhood had somebody that everyone else was afraid of. While that may have been true, I hadn't yet learned the meaning of fear, and it didn't hurt to have an older brother that was known around town. If something was taken from me and I couldn't get it back right then, Art and I would have it back by the next day. Bullies knew who their targets were. They were really cowards whose barks were usually worse than their bites.

લ૭૭

Deno had some setbacks in his early years of life. We weren't from the rich part of town; we were an indigent family. It was mostly indigent boys who were often taken away from their families and sent to the farm plantation. In 1952, my brother Deno was sent to the Florida School for Boys at Marianna because of that reason. He only broke the unspoken law of being indigent and Black.

He was never given the benefit of "Due Process." He never stood before a judge. He was picked up and held in a detention center while a judge, who never laid eyes on him, abused their power and signed him into the state school. This was possible because the State of Florida was allowed to break any state and constitutional law they desired. In addition, Florida even changed the laws for minor offenses to those of felonies to make it easier to enslave poor Blacks. I never knew why; it was a mystery to me for years. Now, I know the answer.

Under the Jim Crow law, people of color had no rights, nor did they have any police protection. White people made up the law as they went along; they could hold my brother and me in juvenile custody as long as they wanted, and for reasons unknown to us. Pretty soon, these police pickups were regular occurrences. If we missed school, the truant officer would come and place us in juvenile care. Maybe that's why I didn't have any memories of Holden Street School. I was never there long enough. From these repeated experiences, life seemed like a tumbleweed; trouble kept tumbling into my life for a long, long time to come.

Looking back over the years, Mama didn't understand what was happening to us; the system had already taken a toll on her. She moved us to different apartments around town, even though she couldn't afford it, in an effort to protect us against the hassles from the police.

Having so much trouble early in my life, I thought I was a misfit. Quite honestly, I didn't know what I thought. At the time, I knew so little about life; however, I couldn't see anything we were doing differently from anybody else. Still, we stayed in the system. I did a lot of thinking. I couldn't figure out anything I did wrong. Later in my young life, it didn't take much to get me fired up. I could strike with force, without warning if danger was lurking.

On our second trip to the juvenile detention center, I tried to figure out why they were so cold toward Art and me. I was young, and my knowledge of Jim Crow or the system was limited. The answer seemed to be out of reach. Looking back over the years, it was simple: racial profiling was "one size fits all" for colored boys from the poor neighborhoods.

Most of the time, they wouldn't allow Art to be in the same cell with me. There were other guys locked up in the juvenile center, but again, most of the time I was alone. Those few times when someone was placed in the cell with me, it would be a couple of days before we spoke. The other boys were always calling to each other at the top of their voices. That never seemed right to me. It seemed like they were happy to be there because they seemed to be right at home. I could never understand that. I never saw anything to be happy about while locked up in a cage.

Every Sunday, whenever I was in juvenile custody, a clergy or someone from the church would come and preach to us. I guess they were trying to get our minds right at an early age. At the tender age of ten years old, and after being detained about three times, I had a little problem with that. The Christians were always preaching, "Pray to Jesus. He will heal you, forgive you, deliver you from a fiery hell, and rescue you in your time of need." That didn't happen. I've heard some say, "You have to wait on him. He comes on time. Just call on him continuously." I tried all that. Sometimes I called on Jesus all night long. I called and called. No one answered. Nobody came to help me. So, I was made to think I did something wrong or dirty and filthy.

My mind just couldn't figure out what I did so wrong that Jesus would never come. I prayed, "What did I do Jesus, that you never came to help me?" That's a question I've wrestled with for years, but I kept calling on Jesus even though he never came. The problem was that Jesus looked just like that man who came to beat Art and me. He looked like White Cap, who locked us in jail for two days and who whipped us in the Middleton-Barney Elementary School in Crescent City. He looked like the man who kept locking us away in that juvenile cell and left us there. The same looking man who punished me for not saying, "Sir" or "Ma'am." He looked like the preacher man who was teaching me to call on Jesus. He looked like the same man as the pictures in that bible they brought to me when they told me to put my trust in him.

Mama, bless her heart, she didn't understand what was going on. Her life was a big roller coaster just as much as ours. I believe the only thing she could do was ride the tide and just look on as the big wheel of life kept turning.

I can imagine Mama visiting all of her friends only to hear them rant, "Mable, don't worry about a thing. God will make a way, you'll see. Just keep praying and asking Jesus to help you."

I remember Mama taking us to Shiloh Baptist Church every Sunday. I watched those sisters get the Holy Ghost and dance all over the place, screaming, hollering out, and singing with praise. It wasn't all bad; in fact, sometimes I was spellbound by the carrying on. Art and I wore our Daniel Boone and Davy Crockett shirts; we put our nickel or dime in the offering plate when it was passed along the pew. Mama was a believer and a praying woman. But, after praying and praying, that wheel of injustice did not stop rolling.

CHAPTER 5
Lies

*A*rt and I met Mrs. Alexander one day while walking to the store. She asked us our names as if she didn't already know; she had already picked us up once. It was like she was trying to catch us in a lie. She had been in touch with Mama and was supposed to help her out with some extra help for us. A little later, we found out what kind of help she meant.

She was a thick lady, not fat, but full-figured. She was smartly dressed and seemly well educated. Mrs. Alexander was the truant officer and was a bad, bad lady. Everyone in Orlando knew who she was except Mama, Art, and me. Our older brother, Deno, was sent to the reformatory school for stealing, but this was not known to Mama, who had no idea who had him sent there or for what reason.

Mrs. Alexander was sneaky and fast when she approached Art and me. She knew why we weren't in school. She knew we had been detained in the detention home, and that we were not able to go to school and had just been released that day. Despite this, she had the ability to gain our trust. She was a Black woman who had authority, and after talking with Mama, we thought for sure we had met someone that had our interest at heart.

Mrs. Alexander picked us up that same day. We thought she was someone who cared about us, a friend of the family. We thought she was going to take us home, talk to our mother, and help get us started in school again. We thought she would tell the school we had been in the juvenile home as the reason for our long absence. I believed if the system allowed us to attend school, things would be alright again. Our clothes and necessities weren't the best, but we could get by. I could never understand why we were always targeted for trouble.

We were not ready for what was about to happen. Finally, Mrs. Alexander met up with Mama, who believed in her and believed she wouldn't lie to her. While we were still sitting in her car, Mama came out to meet her. We heard Mrs. Alexander and Mama engaging in a rather calm conversation.

"Well, you know what, Mabel?" she said. "I can take these boys and put them in a school for you. They'll be just fine. They'll have nice clothes, good healthy food, a good education and everything. They'll have a good time, and you won't have to worry about them. They'll be in school, and they can write to you and let you know how they are doing all the time."

"What's the name of this school?" Mama asked. But Mrs. Alexander evaded her question, and Mama didn't follow up.

"Oh yes, Mable, it's a nice school. A lot of boys go there," she continued in an even more convincing way. "They can play basketball and all kinds of sports. Ya know, boys like that kind of stuff, Mabel. They'll be okay. They need to finish school, and they'll grow up to be good, fine, young men."

"I won't have to worry about them?" Mama said.

Mrs. Alexander shook her head. "No, Mable, you won't have to worry about them," she said before giving Mama a reassuring smile.

Well, that sounded pretty good to Mama. She was so trusting of people. She was a good person and believed everyone thought like she did. Mama was tricked into giving us to Mrs. Alexander, but Mrs. Alexander fooled me too. What she was telling Mama sounded like a pretty good deal to me also.

I thought about what Mrs. Hawkins told us about having a high school education just to get a job as a ditch digger. I thought, if I got a good education, I could help Mama. I already knew what hard work was like from working with Daddy in the fields. All of that was *hard* work. I didn't want to work like that again or grow up to be a ditch digger. My ten year old mind told me with all that education, I could grow up to be someone to be looked up to.

Mrs. Alexander was telling Mama she was going to put us in a place where we could finish school. *Yeah*, I thought. *That sounds pretty good. Maybe there is something to this thing about calling on Jesus. Shoot, Jesus did come after all!* I wanted to see him. Maybe he came while I was asleep. Maybe he came when I was in the detention center. *Okay*, I continued thinking, *Mama always said for us to pray when we were alone.* Those Jesus thoughts had taken control of my mind.

The conversation between Mama and Mrs. Alexander was muffled in the background of my thoughts. Mama was smiling and listening. Anyway, Mama always said, when we were in trouble, pray and tell Jesus about it. He knows our pain, but he wants you to tell him about it, and then you'll see Jesus come and take all of your pain away because he loves you. He will come.

In my little mind, I was ready to go and get that education now so I could come back, be a man, and help Mama. I was tired of those people putting me in juvenile detention homes for doing nothing.

Mama told Mrs. Alexander, "Now, that smallest one can have a little temper sometimes if they mess with him."

"Don't worry about that," Mrs. Alexander said. "They can straighten that out in no time. Don't worry about it; he'll be okay."

I hated to leave Mama, but I believed when we came back home, she wouldn't have to worry anymore. That's the way Mrs. Alexander made it sound. I thought all that bad life would be over if Mama let us go. Art and I sat silently in the car and looked over at Mama and smiled.

Mama turned back to Mrs. Alexander. "Well, ya know I can't do nothin' wit' 'em, like help 'em wit' da school lessons. I ain't got the education like y'all got. Workin' on my kinda job, we're just makin' it, but dey deserve mo'. Dey are good boys, but dey daddy passed away, and every time you look around, dey be puttin' 'em in dat home. I don't know why, but dey do. Like a lot of folk 'round hea', we don't have extra money to buy a lot of stuff, but we're eatin' and sleepin' like everybody else. Dey knows I love 'em and gon' always want the best for 'em."

She leaned down and eyed us in the car. She smiled, took a deep breath, and looked at Mrs. Alexander again. "Okay," she said. "So, if you can put 'em in school so dey can have everythin' dey need, and I won't have to worry 'bout 'em, y'all just take 'em and let 'em finish school. Dat way dey won't have to worry 'bout bein' picked up all da time."

Mrs. Alexander wore glasses and spoke softly; she was very street smart, and she seldom missed her intended target. I think that her kind approach made her so effective.

We were excited and waved to Mama through the open car window, but as soon as we were out of her sight, we were told to roll the window up.

I wasn't too surprised when Mrs. Alexander drove us back to the juvenile detention center. Where else would we stay until we left for the school? I thought.

The next day, Mrs. Alexander visited the judge and had court orders signed to send us to that new school.

This is a copy of a section of the orginal enrollment register for the Florida School for Boys in 1957. Only the names of myself and my brother Arthur are highlighted here. Referred to as colored boys.

PART II
FLORIDA SCHOOL
FOR BOYS
AKA
ARTHUR G. DOZIER
SCHOOL FOR BOYS

CHAPTER 6
A New Reality

*M*y birthday was in April, and we were in the juvenile home waiting to be transferred. The next thing I knew, it was May 10, 1957, and we were going from the detention center to that new school. My brother, Art, and I left Orlando and traveled in a state car together. I had just turned eleven years old. That ride took all day; it seems like it did anyway. Many things were on my mind; I didn't know what to expect. I thought, *we're on our own, going to be educated so we can be somebody one day. Boy, Mrs. Alexander sure is nice to look out for us.*

Over four hundred miles later, we finally stopped at this place. Of course, I didn't have any idea how far that was; one thing for sure, we rode and rode all day. Talk about not seeing that many people in the world, the sights at this place were a shock to me. There were several other boys already there. I saw more people than I had ever seen at one time.

I was scared to death, but I tried not to show it. If this place was a school, it was really pretty, and it was a big place. I had to like this place because there was no way I could find my way back home. I didn't know what to expect, and I didn't speak much, but my mind was busy. We were on our own, and we were going to receive a great education. One day we would be somebody. We just didn't know if this was the school or if there was another one, but I knew we'd find out pretty soon.

We arrived late in the evening, that first day. The guys were getting ready to eat supper. The superintendent, Mr. Mitchell, was waiting in his office for us to arrive. He was a distinguished looking White man; his hair was receding, but what was left of it was parted down the middle. I remember him looking like a high ranking member of the KKK from back in the day. I had heard the people back in Crescent City talking about how the Klan looked, and now I was seeing one for myself. This was just me guessing, but I didn't know for sure.

There was also a teenage Black boy, dressed in white pants and shirt and wearing a black belt. This was the office boy's uniform. He was also the errand boy.

Mr. Mitchell had a few words with us, telling us about the rules and instructing us to stay out of trouble and so on and so on. I was too tired to hear or understand him. He gave us a little package with some stuff in it: a toothbrush, a bible, and a small book, along with a few other items.

The office boy was waiting to escort us to our assigned cottages. There, we were supposed to join the other boys and eat the last meal of the day. I was assigned to Robinson Cottage. The office boy dropped me off first. I was introduced to a Black man named Mr. Ellis, who was the cottage father. Then Art was hurried off to the cottage where he would live.

Mr. Ellis showed me my bed (a narrow bunk) and locker. Then I had a few seconds to put my stuff away and fall into a line formation with the other guys in the cottage to walk to the chow hall.

The cottage, the chow hall, and all the boys were such a new experience; this was a world I didn't know existed. Could this place be the school Mrs. Alexander was talking about? I shook my head. We are just staying here tonight, I told myself.

After supper, we walked back to the cottage in that same straight line formation. Mr. Ellis was waiting for me to return. "I know Mr. Mitchell gave you a handbook of rules," he said. "Remember the rules in that book. I don't care whether you can read it or not. If you can't read, you better get someone to read it to you. It could save you a lot of grief." He stared at me with piercing eyes as he spoke. "Okay, look here, boy." While still looking at me, he pointed to my bed. "This is how I want this bed to be made," he said. Then he showed me how to make my bed. Some of the other fellows stood quietly around and watched.

Mr. Ellis went over every step of the procedure in great detail. "You make your bed every day, boy. Every day! Do you understand?" His tone of voice was course and stern, and he stared at me as he drilled home his instructions. "The rules start here," he said. "Listen, boy, if you wet the bed, what do you do about changing the covers?"

I stood staring up at him with wide eyes. He could see I didn't have an answer. He shook his head. "Boy! You strip them sheets off the bed. Then take them down that hall." He turned and pointed in the direction I should go before looking back at me. "Put them in the dirty linen cart and get two clean sheets off the shelf. Then go get that bed made." He stared at me again like I had already wet my bed.

I nodded and said, "Yes, sir!"

"Oh, and one more thing . . . everyone has a locker and a combination lock. This is important. Keep your area clean! You hear me?" He never altered his firm tone.

"Yes, sir!" I responded. I glanced at the other guys standing around. When Mr. Ellis turned to leave, one of the guys spoke to me, "Man, you alright?" I was alright but speechless.

Then another skinny guy said, "Man, where you from?"

"I'm from Orlando," I said.

Another guy said, "Man, I'm from Orlando too. Where you stay in Orlando?"

"I live by Holden Street School," I answered.

"Oh! Okay, homeboy," he said.

I agreed, giving him a straight look and nod. "Okay," I said, but we didn't know each other. A couple of the guys mumbled to themselves as they walked away, and another couple of guys returned to the dayroom area, while others went outside and sat on the steps.

I got by pretty good that night. There were a couple of guys in my cottage from Orlando. I wondered if Mrs. Alexander was looking out for them too. Seeing them didn't ease my mind much. I needed to wait until the right time or catch one of them by himself to ask about

Mrs. Alexander. But then I did ask one guy form Orlando about how long I would be there before leaving to go to the other school. His answer was quite surprising.

"Another school? Man, this is the only kind of school I know anything about. If you think I'm kidding, man, ask some of our other homeboys, they'll tell you. Ain't no other school! Somebody really fooled you, boy. You didn't know you were staying here, man?"

Dang! I didn't know what to think. It seemed like my world came to an end. I had to sit and think for a few minutes. *This is it?* I thought. I was one mad cat. I could have killed Mrs. Alexander. Why did she lie? Mama put her trust in that upper-class lady; still, she fooled her and us. The real pain came from the realization of betrayal from Mrs. Alexander, whom I wanted desperately to believe in, from Daddy dying, and from Jesus who never really came to help me.

She never told Mama she was sending us to the Florida School for Boys. Deno was sent to this deadly place in 1952. It happened after she and Daddy were separated. Mama said she only heard Daddy sent Deno to that school. Mrs. Alexander said we would be attending a good school. I remember hearing Mama asking her the name of the school. Mrs. Alexander never told her. The truth was, Mama, didn't know she was sending us to a possible death camp.

What can I say? I thought the same thing Mama did. I thought we were going to a great school to get a good education. She stole us from Mama with her lies. She deceived Mama from the very start. She was the truant officer, and she intended to send us to the Florida School for Boys.

Mrs. Alexander never needed Mama's approval; she was working for the state of Florida. She knew there was a great possibility that one of us, if not both, might not make it back home. She was the law. She was responsible for 96% of the young Black boys from indigent families in the Orange County, Florida area to be sent there. She also knew it was a modern-day slave plantation, and she knew it was segregated for little Negro boys. How many of them ever returned home is still a mystery. All the good feelings I had about this person, who I thought cared about us, were now crushing me. I was more hurt because the person who I thought Jesus had sent was the devil in disguise.

Mrs. Alexander was a member of the Black middle class, with a wanna-be upper-class mentality. She considered us to be the nobodies, the unequal, and we shouldn't be the visible children of her very own neighborhood.

I wondered if Mrs. Alexander had anything to do with my brother, Deno being sent here. She knew there was one way into FSB, and two ways out, the front door or the grave. She knew about the missing boys.

CHAPTER 7
Time to be a Man

I was officially assigned to Robinson cottage, and then I was off to visit the doctor. A job assignment and school class needed to be scheduled. School attendance was on an odd/even schedule. If my work detail was on the even days, I would attend classes on the odd days. Then I had to get my hair cut, and next was the ordeal of taking more shots than I could ever imagine; my arms were so sore I could hardly move them. After a week of registration, it was obvious we were at the Florida School for Boys. I hadn't seen Art since the day we arrived.

Everything around me belonged to the unknown. How could anyone in this situation not feel alone, left out, and forgotten? It was during these times I realized I couldn't hold back my tears any longer. I cried on the inside, enough tears to drown in when there was no visible evidence of crying on the outside.

It was a necessity that everyone my age gained knowledge pretty fast. This journey was going to be a job and a tough one, not a joke. From the way things were, there was no time for play, and I didn't want to.

"Bedtime!"

That was my time to unwind and relax that should have resulted in sleep, but sleep never came that easy for me. I buried my face under my sheet because it was a place to think things over; it was the cover for my thoughts. Most nights my thoughts took me away from this school/plantation, but not necessarily to happier times. My young mind pondered the misunderstanding and confusion that played there. Mrs. Alexander was always present, and so were White Cap and the teachers and the principle involved in that school beating.

Now I laid in my bunk at this slave camp. Somebody said we were young slaves, and it was no secret that some boys never returned home. I believed that, because guys would be missing in the morning – guys I remembered seeing in their bunk the night before. The cottage father said their mama came to get them. I don't think their mama would come to get them at night while everybody was asleep. I didn't know what happened to them. Maybe they were the boys that never returned home.

Memories of Daddy were always with me, but stronger at night. They were soothing and gave balance to my misery, especially during those times when memories of Mama's words would sting. Every night I laid in my bunk and remembered the words Mama yelled out from frustration. She and Daddy split up, and Mama took Art with her. Deno was away at the reformatory school, and Lillie Mae was with my aunt. Louise, Luvenia, and I went with Daddy.

I kept thinking if Mama had known better, she wouldn't have let Mrs. Alexander take us without a fight. She couldn't have known this place was like this. We were in a work camp that was not much different than some of the places I saw while on the road, except we couldn't leave without being beaten to death. Mama knew Mrs. Alexander was the truant officer. All the people in the neighborhood knew of her sneaky, conniving ways. Did Mama give us up because she just wanted to be free of us, or just me? Was she willing to sacrifice Art to rid herself of me? Naw! I reminded myself she wouldn't do that.

I was a little different from my brother, Art. He had been with Mama all the time and had never left her side. When she was frustrated with life or with having us to look at all the time, she would always look at me and say, "You! You look just like your daddy! Just get out…go! If I could, I would disown you!" She would turn and look away from me. "I wish I could disown all of you. I want to live my life too!" I tried not to put much thought into things like that; it still hurt a little. Louise and Lillie May were big enough to take care of Luvenia and Linda, but Mama got rid of all her boys, even her beloved Art.

I thought about Art all the time, and I wondered if he was at the same "good school" where he could get that "great education." Maybe Mama had her sweet Art back home with her. Did she and Mrs. Alexander plan all this just to get rid of me? I believed my thoughts because they made sense to me. They justified all that was happening to me.

Sometimes, I was left with deep thoughts regarding the way things happened to me. I wanted to believe Mama didn't mean the things she said, and then I wondered why she always said those words if she didn't mean them. Why was she always telling us how low down and dirty Daddy was? I thought maybe she was angry because he left her here with all the weight to take care of us. That had to get heavy sometimes.

I guess it hurt so badly because I loved my daddy. I remembered so little about him, but it was all good, and that was all I had to hold on to.

No, I told myself. I love my mama too. She didn't know what would be happening to us here. She probably thought we are in some study hall doing just that. I never forgot what Mrs. Hawkins said, "Somebody has got to do the mediocre things in life." I just didn't want to be one of them.

Mama thought she was sending us away to make a difference in our lives, but she was actually sending us to a possible death camp. The way things were at this place, our days could have been numbered. Mama didn't know this. I think the thought and possibility of education overruled her judgment. Mrs. Alexander showed the trait of being well compensated for rounding up all under-aged, underprivileged Black boys and sending them to a free labor slave plantation. Why else would she use that tactic on illiterate, indigent Black mothers who trusted her?

I would wake up to the morning bugle, not ever knowing when sleep had come on me and quieted my mind.

CHAPTER 8
The Rules

*T*he Dozier School and plantation had rules, and every rule broken had consequences. There was a behavioral grade system on the plantation. It was explained in the little book they gave us when we arrived. It didn't matter what was in that little book; I could barely read it anyway. Once I understood the system, it went something like this: When a guy first arrived, he was a "Rookie." The guy was given a chance to learn some of the rules, how to follow orders and stay out of trouble. After a short time, they would be given the rank of "Explorer." This rank was still in the learning phase, but the person should be able to understand the rules enough to stay out of trouble.

The next rank was "Pioneer," then "Pilot" and finally "Ace." A person could lose rank by not following the rules. Except for fighting, most of the rules were not that difficult to follow. Fighting got most of the guys a ride to The White House, but sometimes a guy had to fight to defend himself and not be labeled a punk.

It was the unknown rules, the rules the higher-ups made up on the spot that caused a guy to lose rank or be demoted to the rank of "Grub." Grub was the warning rank, the severe punishment rank, the lowest of the low rank, the ride in the Blue Goose rank. Once in the Grub rank, a guy had to have perfect behavior for three months to move up the rank. The school was clever; they beat you as a reminder to never raise up to fight one of them.

A few things got you a fast ride to The White House regardless of rank: running away, refusing to work, touching each other (always stay arm's length behind the person in front of you when inline), horse playing, fighting, and disobeying a direct command. Oh! Eyeballing a staff member's wife; that could get you killed! That was the one thing you just didn't want to do by any means.

Finally, in those first two weeks, things begin to settle down a little. I began to loosen up, and I started looking and listening to get a feel of how the rules worked. We worked so hard in the fields; there wasn't time for much else. We weren't allowed in the barracks until shower time, about 6:00 PM unless it was raining or extremely cold.

Sometimes, I stretched out on the ground just to relieve my body of the pain plaguing my muscles from the strenuous, exhausting crop work. On better days, I would sit around the basketball court or join in whatever activities were going on. This was our free time, even though most of us were too exhausted to join the others. We relaxed on the ground and watched everything that was happening. We watched the bullies attack guys who were afraid to fight, we watched fights break out between bullies, and we listened to the shit being exchanged between guys trying to fend off intimidation from other guys.

No matter how good I tried to be, there was always going to be some guy trying to build his reputation at my expense. I checked out a couple of guys and the wisecracks they made when passing by. This was an attempt to put fear in me, but it only made me angry. It wouldn't be long now before it was showtime. I was challenged to prove myself.

It wasn't long before I realized some of the boys in the cottage were from my area of Orlando. I had wondered where they were. Families moved away all the time, so I never gave it much thought. Now, I was learning the boys from back home were here with me at FSB. When we were back home, I didn't know what happened to them. They just weren't coming around anymore to play and shoot marbles.

To my surprise, they were all here. I didn't talk much, so when I recognized a guy, I didn't say anything because I wasn't sure who they were. Then when they realized Willie (Deno) was my older brother, and he had a reputation, guys opened up to me and my communication got better.

I knew by now the truth about that school Mrs. Alexander was talking about. In reality, it was this slave camp, but in the back of my young mind, I was still wishing and praying I was wrong. I talked to one of my homeboys; we called him Goose. It was hard talking about my dream of another school, especially when I knew the answers to my question. Soon, I would be looking like a damn chump and crying like a got-damn baby, talking about a school I knew by now didn't even exist. Instead of getting with the program, and what was going on, I confided in Goose about Mrs. Alexander. It was during the late evening hour after dinner while we sat at the edge of the basketball court.

"Goose."

"Yeah."

"I'm wondering, man, do you know Mrs. Alexander?" I spoke quickly. I didn't want him to answer until I was finished asking my question. I didn't want to give him the time to tell me the truth. "She sent us here to go to school and to be somebody one day. She told my mama we were going to a 'very good' school and we would get a bad (outstanding) education. Now we are here, my brother and me, and I'm still looking for that hell of a school. Hell, I don't even see my brother anymore. You ever meet her or know who she is?"

"No, man, no!" Then he turned and stared at me. His face held the answers I didn't want to hear. "Mrs. Alexander? That's who sent me here for playing hooky."

"Not going to school?" I asked. "Hey Goose, man, you joking, right?"

"No, I ain't kidding! This is the school," he said. He dropped his head, inhaled, and then exhaled forcefully. "Man, she told your mama that shit?"

"Yeah, she did," I answered. "I thought we were waiting for someone to come and get us and drive us to that school."

"Homeboy, man . . . ain't nobody coming to get you or your brother. She fooled y'all."

She lied! Why did she lie to my mama? Why did I ask Goose anything? I knew she lied. That made me want to fly away from this motherfucker. My thoughts were so loud, I believed I was speaking out loud.

"Man, don't let nobody hear you saying nothing 'bout that. They'll think you tryin' to run away, and they'll kill you here," Goose warned.

"Say what?" I whispered. "I ain't say nothing about running."

"Don't say Mrs. Alexander's name. She lied to a lot of people. Just hearing you say her name, and they'll think you wanna run."

"Thanks, Goose, man." Why did I say anything about that woman? I already knew the answer. *You know what,* I thought, *if I could see that bitch right now, I'd jump up two feet off the ground and jap-slap the shit out of her right in front of Mitchell and Mobley.*

I had no choice but to get with the program. Every day someone was riding to The White House for one reason or another. I didn't know anything about The White House yet, except I was told you don't want to ever "ride" to The White House.

Fear and confusion held a tight grip on me during those early days. There was no place to go; we were trapped on this spacious campus. This 1400-acre plantation didn't appear to be holding us there, no walls or fences. Only imaginary fences had been placed around our minds, and the consequences of moving beyond them were real. I was warned not to try to escape. The entire town of Marianna was also an imaginary fence. If you dared to steal away from the campus, escaping the town was an impossibility. An ass whipping awaited you just for thinking out loud about escaping and your demise could be the ultimate consequence. There was a saying on campus, "No fence on this place. Take off whenever you feel like it. Just remember that idea could be fatal."

I grew up fast. In the beginning, when I was completely green, only a few people would tell me the right things to do. There were others who would rather leave me to try to figure out the way things were done on my own. I was so scared I would do something wrong because I didn't understand the rules, and the next step would be a beating. But there was always someone to come to my aid, mostly a homeboy from Orlando.

All of us had a stolen childhood. Once we were inside that revolving door to the deadliest reform school in America, we were on our own. One week after I was there, I learned how to drop the little boy's mind. Everything we did was equivalent to a man's job. We were transformed from boys to men at the speed of light.

Soon, I learned every new guy had to go through an initiation period. The only guys that had your back were the ones from your hometown, or who you knew before you arrived, but even they expected you to represent and earn your respect. From that moment forward, I learned this whole journey was serious business.

I was the new boy in the cottage, and a lot of the seasoned guys were always looking for a laugh. It was funny when I was in trouble, because I didn't know the routine—for example, what time to line up, what group I was assigned to, where my assigned group would line up. I was joked and played on, and trouble attached to me. One of the guys, Jason, said to me, "Hey man, this ain't your group, that's your group over there. You'd better get in your group!" I didn't know moving from one group to another without being told by the cottage father would cause a problem. The guys laughed when the cottage father yelled at my confused ass. A flinch, or an attitude was a problem which made them laugh at me for the hell of it.

Almost everyone in the cottage belonged to a group of homeboys or were in some small clan. There were a few guys that didn't seem to fit in anywhere. Most often, they were from out of state. Once in a blue moon, someone who'd visit Florida from out of state got picked up in a kidnapping sweep, or from being in the wrong place at the wrong time with relatives or hanging out with the wrong group of guys. All of us in the cottage looked out for each other; that was the way the system worked within the cottages.

There were two guys, Cuffy and Oliver, who I believed were from South Florida. They were the bullies, the bad guys who always started a fight. That made some of the guys afraid to say anything, although they turned out to be pretty good guys. They would always double team the other guy in a fight. Weaklings just took it all the time, scared to throw a 'shift' (snitch, tell what happened), but then they would really get beat up if they were afraid to fight.

I witnessed a fight one day. We were at the cottage, but the reason was unclear as to why they were fighting. The fight broke out near me. I got a chance to see how these guys fought. We never did bump heads, but I thought we would, so it did me good to see what their method of attack was. I saw how Cuffy and Oliver fought. I picked up their style of fighting: swing first, and end it quickly.

It was bad enough feeling terrified all the time, but to be joked on (clowned on) when I was trying to obey, only to be unjustly punished, was more than I could take. Not following the rules to the letter would get you a grade (write up). Those grades would lead to a spanking; actually, it was a damn beating. I never liked being the product of a joke, especially when I would be the one wearing the bloody stripes and ripped skin from a "strop" (a special-made, very thick leather strap like those used to sharpen straight edge razors).

There was a boy in my cottage named Taylor. Every time he passed by me, he had something smart to say about who I thought I was. He thought I was kidding when I told him what I was going to do if he said one more thing to me. He tried me. Without any warning, I swung at him. He got a fairly good whipping before Mr. Ellis got to us.

I was mad, out of control, and I didn't hear Mr. Ellis tell us to stop. I guess I was in a crazy mode and didn't hear the command. That could have earned me my first ride to the White House that night. Mr. Ellis could have had me ride the first time I got in a fight, but he gave me a chance, and a grade (write up) went on record.

The next day there was no saving me; that meant a beating at the White House. My homeboys tried to tell me not to be a hothead, but it happened before I really thought straight. Mr. Ellis had a system in place to settle disputes, and I could've whipped the dude's ass and saved mine at the same time.

I exploded on the guy who joked on me. The fight began. I walked up to the guy and busted him right in the mouth. To say it was all in my favor might not be quite accurate. I went crazy on him without warning. Mr. Ellis had seen me walk over and hit the guy not once but several times. It was not who won, but it was clear I wasn't there to be laughed at. It was all about respect, and I passed the test, quick and fast. The joke that was pulled on me didn't turn out to be the joke he thought it would be after all. He got a busted lip and a big black eye.

Mr. Ellis pulled us apart and asked what happened. Nobody said anything. The cottage father asked the guy I hit what happened. The guy said he was just playing with me, and I walked up and busted him in the face for no reason. I was asked the same question, and I explained that he wanted to get me a grade by telling me to get in the wrong line, and then laughed at me.

"He didn't get you in trouble," Mr. Ellis said, "you got yourself in trouble when you hit him. I saw what happened. You were just going to beat him up? You ain't been here three got-damn months, and you're going to beat somebody up? Tell that shit to Mr. Mitchell at the office tomorrow. Now get your ass in line. The way you're starting off, you'll be here for a while, boy."

I got a ride to the White House.

CHAPTER 9
My First Ride

*W*hen someone was called to ride, everyone else was so quiet you could hear a rat piss on cotton. Usually, the office boy, who was also the runner boy, came around to your classroom just before school would end for the day and handed the teacher a list. It was a time of self-searching. Everyone seemed to be thinking back, asking themselves if they had gotten a grade earlier and wondering whose names would be read from that list. I knew I had messed up, but that didn't stop me from praying my name wouldn't be called.

Your homeboys, as well as all of the other guys who had taken the ride before, spoke with a single voice. "Hey Hunt! Man, don't turn it loose! Don't turn loose the bed!" they said. The warning came from many voices, but I heard it as if they all were speaking the same words at the same time. "Man, if you turn loose the bed, they will make the other boys hold you down and start the beating all over again!" They'd repeat the warning over again.

"Hold that bed!" Goose said. He knew if I turned the bed loose, it would be a rough road to travel.

I nodded. "Okay, man, I heard you. I'll hold it. I believe you!" At that moment, anger was strength. I was an eleven-year-old Dozier plantation boy about to ride, and all

I could think about was Mrs. Alexander's lies. If only my hatred for that woman could kill, she would take her last breath the moment I took the first blow.

That afternoon, I knew I was facing a possible death sentence at the White House. At least that's what it sounded like all over the campus. When the teacher received that list from the office boy, we sat with our closed eyes praying we didn't hear him call our name. With a deferred prayer, we would leave the class with the office boy. It was all over but the crying.

Besides me, there were about four other boys who were called out. When we got to the office, we sat on a little bench by the door. Mr. Mitchell called me into his office and said, "This is your second write up; that's why you're here today."

I said, "Yes, sir."

"I'm placing you in the Grubs. A Grub write-up means that you're a problem. Have a seat out there."

He spoke briefly to all five of us. I returned to the bench and waited. Mr. Mitchell walked out of his office and said, "Okay, load up."

When we stepped out of the office, Mr. Mobley was waiting, standing near the car. He was a huge Black man who everyone on the Black side knew as a man who wasn't to be fooled with. He opened the back door, and all of us piled into the back seat of what was called "The Blue Goose." It was about a 1953 Ford sedan that had been painted a light blue, and a round State of Florida seal was stuck onto the front doors. This was "the ride" the guys spoke of – the fearsome Blue Goose that transported terrified boys to the torture house.

When the Blue Goose cruised past the guys, they were staring at the car, just looking to see us and confirm who was in the ride. The trip wasn't too far, although it seemed like a long way. It was only across the street from the Black side of the campus. I didn't realize it was that close until then. The White House could actually be seen from the road if you knew what you were looking for.

That day at the White House, Mr. Mobley got out of the car and opened the door. He stood to the side and quickly pointed his finger at us. We got out and marched toward the house of torture.

In the mid 1950's this building was dingy and dirty white, trees were grown up around it, windows were broken at the rear side door, grass was overgrown...you wouldn't have recognized it as a useful building. Many were beaten to the brink of death in that White House, aka torture house or ice cream factory. That is where my heart stopped for a split second from the sharp pain. When the fan was on, the screams couldn't be herd outside.

Our eyes searched the outside of the dingy white house, and then we stepped inside. I shook a little with fear.

My eyes widened as we entered the dimly lit interior. A foul, unfamiliar odor was present; the smell was like none other.

The first time I was taken inside The White House was an experience that is difficult to explain, even as I write this account. The interior of the building was cold, old, and scary, and my insides trembled with fear.

As we walked inside, Mr. Mobley stopped at the first room on the right and pointed at the bed inside. It was dirty and spotted with what seemed to be dried blood. Splatters of blood were on the wall as well. The walls and ceiling were like something out of a horror movie, and I was about to find out why.

Black and White boys were not allowed to be beaten in the same room on the same nasty, narrow little bed. Although I was never acquainted with any White boys, it was said they suffered the same kind of punishment as the Black boys. Black boys sat on the White boys' bed while waiting for their turn to be beaten, and vice versa.

Mr. Mobley told us to sit down, and Mr. Mitchell spoke to all of us. "We don't like' havin' ta bring y'all over here, but dis is da last option. I don' wanna beat y'all like' dis. I know y'all don' like' it. When ya learn ta do what ya told, ya won't have ta go through dis, but ya will do as ya told while ya at dis school." He turned and spoke to a couple of other boys. "Y'all been hea befo'. Ya know wat ta do."

Mr. Mitchell had a southern White man's accent, and his speaking voice was light. Me and two other boys were terrified. We were new to The White House, and Mr. Mitchell addressed us again. "If ya don't hol' dat bed, an' ya turn it loose, we'll hol' ya down an' start beaten ya all ove' agin, ya hea' me?"

I was in a state of panic. I was so scared, my hands and legs were trembling.

"Yes, sir," we mumbled.

"Whatcha say, boy?" he asked again.

"Yes, sir!" we answered in louder voices.

Mr. Mitchell looked at us, deciding which one of us would go first. I hoped he wouldn't pick me, but he did. "You first," he said.

"Yes, sir," I said in my quiet voice. I was so scared my legs were hardly able to support my weight because they were shaking so bad. I took fifteen to twenty steps toward the room across the little hallway. Fear covered me like a shadow, but I knew I was too far gone to turn around. I entered the dingy little room.

Mr. Mitchell gave his speech to make us feel that something we did was so wrong that we deserved every bit of what was about to go down; therefore, the torture was justified. He turned this loud fan on, and the sound made a "woo-woo-woo-woo," noise.

I stood near that little one-person bed. It was scary looking. The mattress was almost black with filth and spots of blood. I thought the foul smell must be the smell of dried blood and pee. My smell senses couldn't identify what else the odor could possibly be. I frowned silently said, "Lord is this where we die?" The chicken-feathered stuffed pillow rested against the metal headrail. The bed had been pushed close to the wall. The pillow looked shiny like dried snot and slobber was on it.

I didn't know what to think; I never saw anything like this. I started to pray; *Lord, don't let them kill me.* I was petrified with fear and still trembling, hoping I didn't turn loose the bed. Thoughts raced through my mind – *I'm about to die, please, Lord, please, don't let me die.* My mind said *run!*, but I looked around, and there was nowhere to run. I couldn't run. I was in a little room—one way in, one way out.

Mr. Mobley was about 250-plus pounds. He yelled at me, "Lay on the bed! Head on the pillow and look at that wall!" My heart was beating fast and hard. The other four guys were in the other room, waiting to hear what would happen to me. He didn't let me see what he was going to flog me with. The thick belt shaped like a leather razor strop was hanging on the wall. He shifted his stance and got into position to take care of business. He was heartless and at ease. That industrial fan blew to muffle the sounds. Mr. Mitchell, a cold-blooded White man with a thin hillbilly voice, stood there watching as the beating got underway. "Lay your head down! Look at that wall, I said! And don't turn that bed loose!"

My heart was pounding fast and hard like it would jump out of my chest at any moment. I didn't see it coming. I heard a movement and suddenly, BOOM!! That first lick hit me with so much force, it seemed like it drove me into that bed at least two inches. It was like an electric charge to my brain. I didn't remember to scream because my brain was trying to process what had just happened to me.

In my mind, I heard, "Nigger, you betta not turn that bed a-loose!" BOOM! The leather strop with the silver dollar embedded at the end of it pounded my little body. BOOM! BOOM! The blows kept coming.

I was sweating, twisting, trying to move, and time the licks. My voice was trembling, my whole body shaking, and I was praying. I started to moan and groan in a loud voice. Then I started hollering out in a loud voice from deep in my gut. The sounds were coming out through my nose. I was huffing and puffing through my nose and from my gut. I remembered to call on Jesus to come and get me. *Save me, Lord, stop the pain! Mama, please save me! Daddy, could you make them stop?*

I was taking short little breaths, saying in a low tone, "Please sir, don't hit me no mo. Yes, sir! Yes, sir!" I realized why the pillow was the way it was. My nose was snotty; I was slobbering and crying into that pillow.

All my strength was gone now. I don't know how many lashes I received. The pain was unbearable. I left my body; I could see Mr. Mobley showering the blows down on me with all his might. I lost count of the blows that connected with my body and watched Mr. Mitchell scratch the floor with his shoe. Finally, Mr. Mobley said, "Get up!"

Lord, I died that day. I know I did. When I got up, it felt like there were two of me. My back parts were so heavy I didn't know what to think. All I heard was, "Stand in that corner and face the wall!"

I remember every blow of that whip against my body; the pain was excruciating. It was said I would remember that strop, the beating, and the power of each blow to my backside and legs, as being unforgettably painful. *GOD* has allowed me to try and express the pain that stopped my heart for a split second to tell the world. I know what it was like, but I still can't describe the depth of it. My brain didn't protect me from that shock. I will always remember the burst of pain from that leather weapon pounding thunderous blows against my backside and legs, separating the muscles in the flesh. These memories always reduce me to chills; I flinch with the memory of each blow. I don't wish that kind of pain on *anyone*.

The guys who suffered the torture inflicted in The White House were greatly lacking in their ability to describe it; it was impossible for them to express their experiences of the real torture inflicted inside those walls. It was impossible for me to imagine that picture in my head. I heard their stories, but I didn't believe anything so far beyond my little imagination of pain. With all the talk going on about The White House, I still didn't understand what I was in for until that day came.

This may sound crazy, but in all the slave explanations I've heard and read, I never heard anyone describe the pain felt when Massa beat a young boy within an inch of his life with a man-made whip tailored to the hand of the destroyer.

That beating of the flesh couldn't be explained by Jesus himself. When the Romans beat Him with a cattail whip, every lash pulled meat from his bones. What man can explain such pain? Let me describe The White House beatings that way.

Mules that plowed in the fields didn't suffer the abuse they administered to our bodies. It was a pain that charged your brain without warning, although you knew it was coming.

My butt and the back of my thigh felt like they were on fire and a big hard ball had been embedded into my flesh. My body throbbed like an infected tooth. I had an out of body experience in that White House. I believe I honestly left my body because the pain was so severe. I had no idea how many lashes I got.

Fear of touching my own body set in. My butt was so swollen, I was afraid it had split open and I would bleed to death. I was in trouble. I had seen other guys who ran away. They returned with split open wounds looking like big blisters that had burst, allowing their flesh to ooze out.

When Mr. Mobley and Mr. Mitchell took us back to the cottage, I tried to look bold, like things weren't so bad, but I was dying inside from the pain. It took a week or so before I could sit down straight. Some of the guys had to have a pillow to sit down the first day or two. The guys who were in that condition were not a laughingstock, because we all knew it could be any one of us at any given time.

I promised I wouldn't put myself in a position to visit The White House again. I constantly asked God for help. For the life of me, I couldn't see what I did so different from anyone else. My homeboys began to see the unnecessary write-ups too. The staff members and cottage fathers watched my every move. I didn't think I would ever leave there alive. I didn't joke a lot and didn't care to be joked with; however, I wasn't the monster they tried to make me out to be.

CHAPTER 10
New School Days

*7*he school was nothing like a public school. I firmly believe The Florida courts sent us there for a purpose. The reform school curriculum was handwritten by the juvenile judge who sentenced us to this so-called school. The real purpose was camouflaged by the concept of the word "school," meaning a place where you'd expect to be educated.

The true purpose of *this* school was that of a segregated farm, a slave plantation for teen and pre-teen colored boys who were the free laborers that actually ran and worked the whole plantation, and the other profit making businesses at the school. The State of Florida gave the school rights to keep its young boys until age twenty one, or until legally released by the school. The State of Florida *owned* us. I was held in the system at ten years old and became a field hand at age eleven. I was a ward of the State of Florida.

I was assigned a school schedule. If Monday was a school day, we would attend school three times that week. If Tuesday was the first day of school, we were only allowed two days of school that week. The system was based on even or odd days. I was tested and assigned to the third grade, where I would remain for my entire stay at the school.

Mr. Johnny Evans was our teacher. He was a Black man of regular size with big eyes, and they stayed red all the time as if he drank a lot. We called him J.D. for "Johnny Drunk." No matter how he looked, J.D. had an important role to play in this system. He had a thing for writing; sometimes, we would spend a half-day just writing cursive out of an alphabet book. Once a week, while in J.D.'s class, we had to write a letter home to our parents.

Whether we could read or not, we had to send a convincing letter home. For those who couldn't read or write a letter in their own words, a letter would be written on the board for us to copy, and each week J.D. changed up the wording of the lies.

I will always remember the letters we were forced to write. For most of the guys, this was the only contact with their homes and families, and they were forced to lie. The impact of this activity will always remain with me. The body of those letters written sixty-three years ago read something like this:

Dear Mother,

How are you? I hope all is well. Tell everyone I said hello. Today is Monday, and I am in school. We are taking our reading class today. It's good to be in school. We are learning a lot.

As this letter leaves me, I am doing fine. We had a great time this weekend. We went to the movie and watched two pictures. When we got back, we stayed outside until bedtime.

I can't wait to come home. My grades are getting better. I've been staying out of trouble for a while now. My cottage father said I will be able to go home soon. I sure hope so. I'm closing my letter, but not my love.

Your baby son,
Richard

Every letter written by every student would be read and inspected. It was Mr. Evans' main responsibility to make sure the letters were approved before mailing them out to the parents every Monday or Tuesday.

My mother never knew when I was beaten within an inch of my life. She didn't know when my body was so bruised and sore that I had to take my time just to sit down, or how I suffered physical pain for weeks on end. I had to write lies like this with pain in my heart.

I was assigned to work as a slave in the fields on the farm. The wakeup bugle sounded at 5:30 am, and we had to hit the floor running. It seemed like daybreak always came so fast. My body would still be tired; I ached from just walking.

We were definitely slaves to this system. The animals were allowed to rest, but we weren't. There were so many Black boys slaving on the farms, I believed they would've had to close the place down if they didn't have our stolen and free labor.

At the end of our workday and after the dinner hour, we weren't allowed to enter the cottage to rest. We laid around outdoors; some of us were under the trees, some sitting and resting on the benches, and others were lying around the basketball court. Then, there were those guys with enough energy to play basketball. I believed they played just to give their bodies a relief from the day's stress.

We were forced to remain outside of our cottages in the cold or the heat of the evening sun. Those fifteen hour days were torturous before being allowed to shower and hit the bunk.

By day's end, after I made it to my bunk to rest, I couldn't quiet my mind. I would be so keyed up, I just couldn't get my brain to settle down. The thought of everyday life on the plantation sometimes made it seem like I hardly went to sleep, and by the time the bugle blew in the morning, I didn't remember falling off to sleep.

On my school day, the beauty of the new day meant time off from slaving in the field. My body would enjoy the full twenty four hours of relief from the agonizing heat or record-breaking cold. It was a time of freedom from muscle strain and pain. Still, I couldn't escape my fatigue, which made it very hard to stay awake in class.

I was so tired all the time, it was very hard to remain alert. When I dozed off in class, I always got caught simply because it was almost impossible not to be seen. J.D. would walk up and touch me. I never remember seeing his approach. Next, he would beckon for me to come to the front of the room in view of all the other guys. He had a twelve-inch wooden ruler that he used to beat the knuckles of my right hand until I couldn't close it. I wasn't allowed to change hands for a small relief of his harsh punishment. My fingers would stand straight out, swollen, and trembling with pain. Now, *that* brought tears to my eyes. The tears rolled down my face, not from the pain of my hand, but the thought in my heart of wanting to kill somebody for the price I was paying for doing nothing wrong that I knew of.

J.D. would say, "This will help you remember to go to sleep at night!" This was his punishment for all the guys he caught sleeping or dozing off.

I couldn't believe this was that great education Mrs. Alexander promised my mother. If the teachers had been allowed to give us a quality education with math, history, English grammar, reading, and the trades, we would have stood a much better chance of success in life. We would at least have an opportunity to earn a GED, and that would have been a damn good start as far as an educational foundation was concerned.

It was a fact that the education the Black boys received was inferior to that received by the White boys. The White boys received credentials documenting their educational achievements, as well as certifications in marketable trades.

In addition to a few other resources available to J.D., he used the Holy Bible as the basis of most of our lessons during my two year stay. We were taught a lot about the bible. We were made to memorize a variety of bible verses, and then we were left to our own interpretation. It was natural that when reading a book like the Holy Bible, I could not apply the verses to my current situation. I was just a young boy.

Psalm 100:1-2   A Psalm of Praise.
1. Make a joyful noise unto the Lord, all ye lands.
2. Serve the Lord with gladness: come before his presence with singing.

We were confined to the State of Florida's reformatory system. Slavery concepts and behaviors were expected and reinforced. We were expected to bow down to the masters who were perceived as all-powerful staff and make a joyful noise and be glad.

These are the same concepts that were drilled into our slave ancestors for over four hundred years. This was the intended message that was beaten into us, and that made the difference in our compliance.

I Corinthians, 13:11
When I was a child, I spoke as a child, I understood as a child, I thought as a child: but when I became a man, I put away childish things.

This verse was important to the staff. Teach them to put away child's play and work like a man. It's about your father's (Florida School for Boys) business on this plantation.

Luke 6:27-28 (Jesus said)

27. But I say unto you which hear, love your enemies, do good to them which hate you, 28. Bless them that curse you, and pray for them that despitefully use you.

It was hard to believe that we, teens and preteens, were expected to understand and follow the teachings of Jesus from Luke 6:27-28. We were slaves and treated worse than the animals we cared for. How could we love, forgive, and pray for our tormentors? As young boys, we worked like oxen from "can see in the morning until can't see at night." I knew this system was wrong, and love and forgiveness was impossible. My mind just couldn't accept that.

We worked in weather too hot for the bare head, and in the winter too cold to function, but we survived because we didn't know any better; we didn't know we had been rounded up as cargo and shipped off as free labor slaves and were the property of a secret society. I named it "Florida's best kept secret," where we were forced to function under the fear of severe beatings and death. What else would make a person work under these conditions?

We were forced to work, and they were trying to brainwash us to love the slave masters of this boys' school/plantation, turn our other cheek to the abuse we took over and over again, and give those devils anything they asked for—and to do it joyfully.

"No! No! No!" I told myself I had to learn and recite these verses because it was a part of J.D.'s curriculum, but I didn't have to believe in them. I couldn't believe Mr. Evans, this Black man, a descendent of slaves himself, wanted us to believe these were the teachings we were supposed to bestow on our master (State of Florida).

Of all Mr. Evan's teachings, there was something that stood out to me. He never used the color of the characters he was talking about, including the description of Jesus. Mr. Evans made sure we understood these saying, Isaiah 52:13-15 and Isaiah 53:1-3, which implies that beauty by standard is an allusion. He taught us the person with the beautiful soul and heart might possibly be the ugliest person you know in outward appearance. Jesus was not a beauty for the eyes to behold. I got this understanding from the messages, even though pictures showed us that Jesus' appearance was that of a beautiful White man.

Later in my life and with extensive reading of the Holy Bible, I came upon the following chapter and verses which described Jesus' character and appearance. During my youth, I couldn't understand how the man who was perfect could be so cruel. At this school, I saw cruelty from most of the staff who resembled the images of the Jesus I was familiar with. The White man with the long brown hair and blue eyes. However, Isaiah 53:1-3 gave me a clear description of Jesus.

Isaiah 53:1-3

1. *Who has believed our report? And to whom is the arm of the Lord revealed? 2. For he shall grow up before him as a tender plant, and as a root out of a dry ground: he hath no form nor comeliness* (NIV translation: - He has no beauty or majesty) *and when we shall see him, there is no beauty that we should desire him. 3. He is despised and rejected of men; a man of sorrows and acquainted with grief:* (NIV translation: - a man of suffering, and familiar with pain) *and we hid as it were our faces from him; he was despised, and we esteemed him not.* (NIV translation – we held him in low esteem).

At that young age, I knew something was wrong. I believed Mr. Evans had a heart after all. There was a time when he gave us a message we could understand. He let us know the religion being taught was inaccurate and wrong, and we were being brainwashed just as our slave ancestors had been.

I realized J.D. could not have worked at this school without knowing of the slave conditions the Black boys were forced to endure, how we were driven to work the farms, the crops, and the slaughterhouse, from early morning to the dinner hour with only a lunch break. None of the White boys were ever assigned these work details.

I wondered why, if J.D. knew of the inequality in the system, in our education, and of the merciless beatings in The White House, why couldn't he allow us a kinder condition in the classroom. I believed his position was only a few levels above us. He was also Black, and his salary could be calculated as slave wages, a fraction of what the White teachers made. He was also being forced to teach a doctrine that supported the brutality we were experiencing. It left me to question why he couldn't just give us a rest period; a power nap could have given us the energy our little bodies needed, and we would have been better students, but that never happened.

None of the staff had feelings for us, at least that's how I felt during my stay. They were mere slaves themselves with a different title, "Negros in Charge." Whether they were in the classroom, barracks, or on the farms, they were just like field Negro overseers, teaching us to be well-mannered peons.

I thought working in the fields with Daddy was hard work, but it was nothing compared to this school plantation. We were made to work sometimes nonstop, back-breaking work, forced by the threat of pain. The White House pain was pain no human can explain. Work was our main purpose for being there, and like slaves, education was not a priority for us. However, I never rode in the Blue Goose (the blue state sedan) to The White House for getting my lesson wrong or failing a test during the two-plus years I was made to stay there.

It was different in J.D.'s class. Maybe he did care. I don't believe he was being cruel all those times he beat my knuckles. He could have given me a "grade" (write up), which would have resulted in a ride. But when I think about it, he could have just given us that rest period. He wanted to give us an education using whatever tools available to him, but was that why my knuckles were beaten for sleeping in class or for being too tired to learn those bible verses? I know he understood the brutality of our slave labor condition; was he so powerless that he couldn't give us a little nap break here and there?

CHAPTER 11
The Farm

*T*he day after a school day, we were back in the fields working. I knew about fieldwork, but I had to learn how to be a slave. On our field workdays, we worked from the time we could barely see daylight, until the time you couldn't, during the shortened winter months.

Our day started right after breakfast; everyone was off to their jobs. The poultry and dairy crew, hog farm crew, tractor crew, plow crew, farm field crew, slaughterhouse crew, laundry/sewing room, and other assignments. I worked in at least three of those places at one time or another.

At first, I didn't realize the jobs I worked in the processing plant, the farm, and cane crew, offered some benefits. I could bring plenty of goodies to the cottage to trade with other guys (bologna, spiced ham, wieners, crackling, cane, sweet potatoes, berries, etc.) for a part of their Christmas gifts and any other goodies they got from home (for example, cookies and candy). I always looked out for my homeboys, and they looked out for me.

Mr. Stevens, a Black man, oversaw the field crew. When a new guy was assigned, one of the more experienced guys would show him how to do the job. The work on Dozier Plantation was hard, and we had to work at a steady pace. It was like we had to move to the beat of a drum. We couldn't take a water break or rest whenever we wanted; that wasn't allowed. We had to ask permission to relieve ourselves. The most important thing of all, we had to meet our daily quotas.

The first thing we had to do in the morning was to sharpen and prepare our job tools, and repair or replace any broken handles. Mr. Stevens would yell out, "We ain't got all day to get these damn tools ready! The mule boys shouldn't beat y'all gettin' outta here! What's the matter, y'all got no sleep last night? Get the lead out of your asses, and let's go! We got a whole got-damn cornfield to hoe today, and I don't plan on being out there all day in the sun doing it! Let's go!"

His hands moved to the beat of his every word while he strutted back and forth. "One other thing . . . y'all seem to forget because I don't usually give any of you a grade when you fuck up on my crew, you don't know who I really am, but that stopped yesterday!" Mr. Stevens did most of his talking in the mornings before we left for the field.

We all looked at each other, wondering what he meant when he said, "That stopped yesterday!"

"Terrell!" Mr. Stevens shouted. "You and James . . . I got y'all's number, the next time y'all see me, you'll know who the hell I am!" Later that day, after dinner, Terrell and James took a ride to The White House. I couldn't believe Mr. Stevens was that angry! That next day of fieldwork, Mr. Stevens told us, "Any time anybody out here picks up a tool toward someone else, I'll have your ass sent to the justice center before God gets the message." That was his way of saying, you'll get sent to The White House before God can hear your prayers.

Everyone found out it was time to get their act right. Mr. Stevens wasn't anyone to joke with either. "We're out here to do a job, damn it! Let's get it done! How many times I told y'all that you talk wherever you want too, except on my job!" He spoke as the authoritative figure that he was. "Let me tell you knuckleheads something right now! I don't feel that good today, and I won't be doing that much talking. Since some of y'all can't seem to shut your got-damn mouths, we are going to work the cornfield today, every inch of it! We will water up when I say we do! We won't take a break in the shade unless I change my mind! I don't have to stand in that sun all day; I can stand in the shade like I'm gonna do today! If one of you fall out from the heat, we'll throw you on the back of this wagon and leave you there until you cool off and get back to work. We will finish this cornfield this evening! We gonna finish that field if we have to stay until nightfall! Alright, let's load up; we got work to do!"

The work was hard, and the blisters on my hands were many. They never really healed because the injuries reoccurred every other day. We were never given work gloves. Mr. Stevens said, "Piss in your got-damn hand, that'll make 'em tough. Ain't no fucking babies on my damn job, and I don't raise 'em!"

So, now I had sore hands and throbbing knuckles from J.D.'s class and sore blisters in the palms of my hand from using the hoe and shovel in the field. No public crying; show no weakness. No one cared about how you felt, and the fellas would play on your weakness.

I had to continue; I had to work through any physical pain. I had to hoe that long row of corn, lift those bales of hay, dig that hole, sling that sling blade, work the fields of all kinds of vegetables, and do whatever was necessary work on every aspect of the farm. We even made fertilizer from the farm animals' dung. We worked the feed, the seed, we hoed, picked, plucked, and pruned, we packed, stacked, piled, and sorted. We were free laborers working at a grown man's pace.

It was long days of hard work, summer and winter, no matter the weather. It was hard times. The gruesome work separated the weak from the strong in the fields, cow pastures, and saga pits. We pulled corn from the stalks for the kitchens of both sides of Dozier, Black, and White. We were depended upon to feed everybody and everything, plants, animals, and humans at the school. We also provided food, for a profit, for the whole town and countryside of Marianna in Jackson County. The locals purchased the meat and produce guaranteed by the slave laborers of Dozier.

The surplus remainder of corn from the summer crop was cut down, harvested with machines, and stored in deep pits for cow feed in the winter. The sour drainage from the buried corn smelled just like liquor, and some of the older guys would drink it, saying it gave them a buzz. It did smell like liquor, and curiosity pushed most of us to try to drink it also.

Burying green corn and storing it for cow feed during the winter months. Once covered, it drained a liquid that smelled like liquor or homebrew. Credited to: Florida Memory from 1957.

Some of our other work details included barbwire repair, making syrup from fresh chopped cane, cleaning ditches, hoeing long, long rows, weeding all kinds of vegetables, bailing hay, caring for the mules, and anything else that didn't require brain usage.

Most of the time, Mr. Stevens didn't ride our backs. He wasn't quick to write you up, you had to do something pretty bad to get written up, but he didn't miss his daily quota either. We had to get down and dirty and get that work done. Working the plow crew taught us a valuable lesson: boys didn't survive in this place. We had to make up our minds to be men because, though we were not grown men, our production was equivalent to that of men.

Young men are plowing a field of corn. Greenville Region, Florida. Credited to: Madison Collection. Memory of Tallahassee, Florida. 1935.

Winter or summer, Mr. Stevens had a quota to meet daily. The winter days at work were some of the worst times I have had. The summer months were extremely hard; the working conditions were very brutal. Cultivating corn and peas in the fields was back-breaking, and it was sweltering. Every morning when we got to the barn, we received our daily work schedule. Sometimes it was a job left unfinished from the day before, mostly because of bad weather. Other than severe and dangerous weather, a full day's work was required.

I remember one particular brutally hot day in the cornfield. It was so hot, the sun was baking our brains. I pulled my shirt over my head to protect it from the extreme heat, and God spared us by supplying a few thin clouds to shade us from the sun. What a blessing from heaven! Two of the guys got dizzy; one of them slowed down, wiping his forehead a lot, and looking up at the sun. He bent over and put both hands on his knees. He just stood still in one place, and somebody hollered out to him, "You alright, man?"

"I think so," he answered. Sweat was popping off him faster than he could wipe it away. He was breathing pretty hard when Mr. Stevens called out to a couple of guys, "Take him over to the shade and let him cool off before he falls out. He'll be alright." He was allowed to sit in the shade for a while before returning to work.

A second guy called out to Mr. Stevens, telling him he didn't feel right, that he felt faint. Mr. Stevens told him to get on over to the shade before he caught fire.

The sun was hot; sometimes, I think it did bake my brain a bit, especially with no cap to protect my head and only my tee-shirt to protect my back. We worked in 90^0 to 100^0 temperatures during the summer months. We worked hard on that farm, and many days I was dog tired when it was time to go in. I could hardly put one foot before the other.

I'd fall asleep in the wagon while returning to the barn in the evenings. Then we had to put the tools up before heading to the cottage. Then, of course, we were not allowed to enter the cottage until after dinner. I would stretch out on the grassy ground for a nap.

The building was open for us if it rained or to use the bathroom. Other than for those reasons, it was a no-no to enter the building until shower time and getting ready for bed. There was no playing around allowed in the cottage.

Mr. Stevens was hard on us, but on those hot summer days, if we didn't tarry, we could get cool water from the hand pump water wells in the various fields. However, there were so many snakes at the edge of the fields, especially under the shade trees where the water pumps were located. Sometimes we could see snakes in the water wells as we drew water to drink.

Pumping water was usually a two man operation; we literally pumped water to drink straight out of the ground. It was an iron pump with a spout on the front and a long neck handle on the back. Usually, a bucket of water would be sitting close by with a dipper in it. This was used for priming the pump.

We had to fill the top of the pump with water to prevent air from seeping by the inside rubber ring. Then, the well would build up pressure to draw water by pumping the handle. Cold water came straight out of the ground. It was cold enough to quench our thirst.

I thanked my God for just making it through those days. For as long as I can remember, I have always felt that everyone had their own personal God, and I still believe that to this day.

My prayer: *Lord, it's me, Richard, again. I know you're busy, Lord, but I need your help. Would you please stop by here? Thank you, Sir. I know you will. You've brought me a long, long way.*

Jobs in the watermelon patch for eleven and twelve year-old boys were excruciating and painful work; cutting and loading those heavy watermelons wore us out. Some of those melons weighed almost fifty pounds, half the weight of some of us. After loading them on the wagon, they would then be disbursed to all the mess halls on campus. We were allowed to eat one or two of the melons in the field.

Mr. Stevens had to report one of the guys on the crew. He wasn't able to do the work. I thought something was physically wrong with him. He was smaller than most of us, and for that reason, he didn't seem to be as strong. He dropped several watermelons and he couldn't stand the heat from the sun. We tried to carry him, but it was apparent he couldn't do this specific job.

Mr. Stevens finally had to report him to the office, asking that Fred not be sent back to the field. That report could have been a recipe for disaster for Fred. The school didn't play that. I think he was from North Florida. I never saw him again. What happened to him because he couldn't do the work was a mystery. We never found out what happened to Fred.

Farm work was backbreaking, from scooping cow manure to chicken poop to be composted and used for fertilizer. It had a stink that baked into your skin, and the fumes from it brought water to your eyes. The stink coupled with the unbearable heat meant people could smell us a mile away.

On the days we worked with the manure and in the chicken coops, we were allowed to shower first. That stink was a punishment to mankind, but the fertilizer was used to enhance the growth of the produce from collard greens to cantaloupes.

CHAPTER 12
The Grave Diggers

*T*he field crew taught the older teenagers how to drive the mules to pull the plow. If we didn't like the work we were assigned, we didn't speak or grumble about it; we had to pretend we liked it. If Mr. Stevens said something to us about our work, we answered him, and we got the job done.

He didn't play about the daily quota. He wasn't quick to write us up, but if he had to report you, the office would send the Blue Goose to pick you up from the field. If that happened, everyone on campus knew what that meant: that person was going to need help after that ride. The deadliest force on the plantation was The White House. That alone separated the little boy's mentality from that of a man's. Only men worked here.

One summer day, we were walking through the cow pasture looking for fences in need of repairing. We were warned to stay in a huddle, close around each other near the fence. Palmetto bushes and manure were pretty much everywhere. Mr. Stevens had just told us not to walk near the palmetto bushes. Suddenly, one of the other guys yelled, "Mr. Stevens, what's that in those palmetto brushes?"

Mr. Stevens shouted, "Get back! Get back! That's a snake!" It was a diamondback rattlesnake, and it weighed about one hundred pounds. We had seen plenty of snakes in the field, but I had never seen a diamondback that big! We killed it and we were amazed to see its rattlers were the size of a jumbo marble.

Every day we were faced with danger in one way or another. We were also the cleanup crew for the dead farm animals. Once, we had to bury a dead mule. The frightening thing was the dead mule had swollen so large that his legs were standing straight out.

It was scary. It looked like the mule was standing up, but laying on the ground partially on its back. That might sound a little crazy, but his skin was also moving. Now *that* was scary. We didn't want to get close to it, but there were no other options, so we walked up to it.

Mr. Stevens told someone to hit the dead mule across the belly with one of the shovels. The carcass was decaying, and the smell wasn't too sweet. Frankly, the damn mule stunk. Being the big man I believed myself to be, I walked up and hit that mule first.

What happened next was unbelievable. Opossums, *many* of them, were moving under the skin and were now running out of its butt hole! I thought of the people who actually ate opossums as a meal when we lived in Crescent City. We learned a lesson about opossums that day: they would eat dead people, too.

We had two work crews all the time. One crew was doing the fieldwork, depending on the season of the year. I never had an interest in farming, and I'm not familiar with what grows at different times of the year. Often the other part of the crew was doing other jobs that were more to my liking, such as replacing fence poles, fixing barbwire, delivering salt blocks, cleaning out ditches, digging holes, and burying animals. There were times when we dug holes but had nothing to put in them. We left them open. We didn't know why we had to dig different size holes, and we didn't ask questions.

We were the earth's cleanup crew. We dug holes and buried the dead animals. We were told when an animal died on the farm, it was our job to take care of it and make sure it was buried, and we did. Many times, we had to make sure to keep the vultures from swarming around and eating the carcasses. Things were done in such a coordinated manner, I sometimes wondered what our real responsibilities were.

As I was writing this memoir, my mind started to uncover some things that were unbelievable and troubling to me. Often, Mr. Stevens took three or four of us to another location to dig holes. Were we digging holes just for dead animals, or were we the real grave diggers for our own dead brothers' graves? Were their bodies dumped into a hole at night? Our assignment was to fill in any open holes the next day.

We didn't know what was in the holes. Whatever was in there was covered with just enough dirt so we couldn't see what it was, and frankly, it didn't matter at the time. We were always looking for an easy day. Some of the holes were rather small and some larger. Since we worked every other day, we thought the crew from the day before dug a hole but didn't have enough time to finish covering it up.

In my young mind, I thought some of the other guys used the tractor and brought the dead animals to the holes—but then, *we* were the ones with the tractor. Mr. Stevens took the whole crew around to different sites to make sure things were done right; the holes were filled in and smoothed over.

Mr. Stevens would say, "We got a hole to dig later today, so put the shovels on the wagon, too." That was considered an easy day during the winter or summer, particularly in the summer. We could take our time digging as we worked in pairs. We could walk off to get water while waiting for our turn to dig.

Two guys had to stay together, and we always had to stay in sight of each other. We could sit down while the other two were digging, and then we would relieve the other two guys. In the winter, we could build a fire to keep warm while waiting to dig. Of the two crews, the even and odd day workers, each paired crew never really knew what was going on; we just did what we were told to do.

Today, I wonder about those holes. Did we dig our brothers' graves? Were they that clever, knowing we were too young to figure it out at the time? We dug the holes, and we filled the holes. Some were half full the next workday. What or who was in the half filled holes? Were any of our missing brothers in there? Were we our brother's keeper? Did we dig their graves? I don't know.

CHAPTER 13
Protect Yourself

*T*here were times when a fight would break out at a moment's notice. All it took was a smart mouth from somebody that the other person wanted to shut up anyway. Sometimes it was just one of those days when nothing went right, or someone got a grade on the job or in school. Perhaps he hadn't heard from home in two or three weeks and was beginning to feel his family had forgotten he was still a part of them. Maybe the little money on the canteen book had run out, or it was just one of those days that nothing seemed to matter, and somebody got their lamp put out (black eye). Aside from the fight, the consequences of your behavior could be painful and could mean a ride.

During those rainy or freezing cold days, we would have down-time where we had more time for thinking. The staff believed this was dangerous to the school, so they came up with activities to keep us busy. Saturdays were general cleanup days; Sundays, church day, and then all kinds of play activities—running relays, playing basketball and softball, you name it. But all the equipment was always hand-me-downs from the White side of the campus, or from other schools.

We had one coach, Coach Smith, who was the coach for the whole school. I have never been much of a sports guy, but boxing and singing had always been in me, though I can't say where it came from. I began to understand I was in FSB for the long haul, and I started to focus on other things like getting the hell out of there alive. Before my journey was over, I saw three or four guys come in and leave, and I was still sitting there. That hurt. I'd always pray;

Lord, it's me again, old Richard needing your help. I don't mean to bother you so much, but I have no one else to turn too. Show me the pathway out of here, and don't let these people take my life. I honestly don't know why I stay in so much trouble. I am waiting on your answer Lord. And Lord, please bless my mother and all of my family. I think some of these other guys also need a little prayer, so please look out for them too. Amen.

On the first Friday of the month after my arrival, the school had a talent show. Mr. Ellis asked if I could sing. I thought I could sing, it was no big deal, I thought most people could sing, so I said, "Yes."

Then he said, "Do you want to sign up to sing for Robinson Cottage in the talent show?"

I didn't know what a talent show was, and I didn't ask. Instead, I straightened my shoulders, looked up at him, and declared, "Yes sir, I want to sing." Those words just came out of my mouth before I could stop them.

Agreeing to sing seemed to change my relationship with all the fellas in my cottage. I didn't know what I was in for. It happened so suddenly, right before the show. I wondered what made me say I would do it.

I sucked in air and thought since I was feeling so blue, I would sing a song about the blues. There were two songs my dad loved, which he used to play all the time on my sister Louise's phonograph. *Blue Monday* by Fats Domino, and *The Things I Use to Do* by Guitar Slim.

That night I was called on stage; the cottage father was standing by me. He told me they were waiting for me to go up. I had no idea what to do, I never saw a stage before, so I did what I saw the person did before me. I sang my heart out in the talent show; I sang *Blue Monday*.

I didn't bring the house down; however, there was some clapping and a little noise. I was glad they didn't boo me off the stage. I was kind of proud of myself. I did a talent show without practice or knowledge of the stage. I didn't know I wasn't supposed to step on the stage in front of two or three hundred people and sing, but I did it.

I don't know where my stage courage came from. I was wondering why everyone was making such a big deal about my singing in the talent show. It must be something about the stage that frightened them, but it beckoned me.

After the talent show, we went back to the cottage. Things were pretty good. The next day was Saturday, and that's when things started happening to shape my stay at The Florida School for Boys.

A few guys I didn't know started saying they were my homeboys. Truly, homeboys were just somebody to carry on a conversation with. Mostly, we talked about our present situations. They were interested in every bit of my past life, including where I had been in my travels. One thing my homeboys did for me, they all watched my back.

I think it was Goose or one of the other homeboys who told me about the things being said about me, like, "He thinks he's something 'cause he sang in the talent show." One of them pointed out a guy doing all the talking.

"Man, we're watching your back, but be careful," one of my homeboys said.

I was thankful to have the homeboys. We took care of each other. We were family. They watched my back, and I looked out for them. They were a steady source of information, like a survival tool. They were with me when I needed them. They told me how to survive being the new guy at the school. My homeboys started filling me in on some serious issues, like telling me what to watch out for and to stay out of trouble. "Look out for 'the shake,'" one of the homeboys said.

The shake was when a boy tried to rub up against another boy with his penis, catching him off guard. They tried that on boys after they sized them up for signs of weakness, and on the boys who were too scared to fight. These boys perceived the light-skinned, mulatto boys with the straight hair as weak because they were the ones who wanted to tell the cottage father everything instead of defending themselves.

There were some fights in the cottage where you would've thought it was grown men tearing up the place. For some, that was their first White House ride. Most of the guys that went to The White House were trying to stay out of double trouble, meaning either dropping to the Grub's level or being beat to the brink of death for defending themselves. After the shake or having to defend themselves, they were like raging bulls. It would take a ride to The White House to cool them down. Then there were some guys who had to go to The White House to be made a believer because they had running away on their minds. How many lives were taken? Only God knows.

They also schooled me about "the feels." That was when a boy tried to feel you on the sly, touching your butt. I was also warned about the shower, how boys would try to get boys to bend over to pick up their soap to look at them from behind. And then there were the boys who wanted to be bullies and intimidate others, only to get a beat down by total surprise.

Your real friends were your homeboys. They would always pull you to the side and tell you what trouble was brewing. They'd give you information on how to stay out of any traps. Other experienced guys who were trying to go home would also tell you how to avoid danger zones as much as possible, but your homeboys had your back. They were like your right hand, and they all stuck together in their click, no matter what.

Your homeboys would advise you if one of us had words with this dude or that dude, not to ask questions; just put their lamp out and then go to duke city (fist fighting), then turn the cottage out, where everyone would stop what they were doing to see who would win the fight. If somebody tried to jump in the fight, the homeboys would jump in too.

I was told to stay away from any boy who was always talking trash and who couldn't fight his way out of a paper sack. These guys should just be avoided because they were not worth the trouble.

The bottom line, the objective was to try and stay out of trouble so that we could go home as quickly as possible. We didn't want to have to ride to the White House for a whipping. They called it a spanking, but actually, it was an attempted murder the way they flogged us. The word "beating" wasn't the term for it. In other words, stay out of the path of The White House because you didn't want to end up there. That was the torture chamber. No mercy!

Mr. Ellis, the cottage father, was a firm man. Nobody pushed over anyone if Mr. Ellis knew it. He was quick to have you get the boxing gloves, and there would be a supervised fight until someone won, or there was no more fight left in you. It was strange, but after all that fighting, we would become friends.

Most of the time, if there was any bullying going on, they would do it in a crowd, and fast while the cottage father was in the building or someplace where he couldn't see what was going on. It was up to the individual to say something if he was being bullied, or to fight back if he was being done wrong. I saw a lot of bullies get a hell of a surprise by trying to bully and couldn't fight.

When I arrived back at the cottage at the end of the day, usually, I didn't want to play. There were more than two hours between dinner and the time we were allowed inside the cottage. My whole body ached. I could barely lift my arms from hoeing a field, lifting bales of hay, or shoveling animal dung for composting. The other guys didn't like to see you quiet. If I didn't want to joke in the evenings, everybody believed something was wrong,

I didn't have the strength to play basketball or chase around the cottage with the other guys. Heck, I wondered where the other boys found the strength. Some of my homeboys sat in circles, "shooting the dozens." I took a deep breath and told myself most of the fellows look content, happy like they didn't have a care in the world. My playing sometimes consisted of a little boxing, especially on the weekends. Sometimes, I'd just muster up a song and sit against a tree, just singing my heart out. That didn't take too much energy.

Most of the other guys respected the field crew, dairy, and other similar crews. I usually didn't participate in a lot of the activities jumping around and playing a lot, especially on workdays. I never was one to feel right at home and be satisfied with being there anyway. An accusation of being labeled a run-a-way could cause someone big problems. Usually, if the person didn't run in a few days of thinking about it, chances were slim to none that they would run at all. Anyway, it would be crazy for a little guy like me in Robinson Cottage to try to run. Where would we go at ten or eleven years old? But some of them tried anyway.

We had to find ways to amuse ourselves to keep from going crazy. I used to like playing The Dozens and telling jokes. Whenever everybody gathered around with different jokes or lies to tell, there I would be also. This was our entertainment; we had to do something to pass the time.

CHAPTER 14
The Bears

*T*he nights were most feared by me for two reasons, bears and bedwetting. Fact or fiction, fear is real. Robinson Cottage was the house closest to the woods. We feared one of them bears might come in the building and get us. We knew the entire grounds didn't have a fence around it to detour the bears away from the cottages.

We heard the stories about the guys that had gone missing, and we were left to assume it was the bears. All the tales about the bears coming in the cottage and taking little boys out in the middle of the night, killing them and the staff finding them in the woods, was a hell of a fear factor.

The cottage father's residence was on the second floor, and the barracks were on the main floor. The cottage lights remained on all night long. I didn't know if this was good or bad because I was in a new place. The lights limited my fear of the dark, but I believed it also made it easier for the bears to see us. Add to that, except for very cold nights, the cottage doors remained open all the time, twenty-four-seven. But when I thought about it, those wooden cottage doors would not have stopped a bear if it wanted to get in.

The area of my bed was my private room. I couldn't turn off the lights, but I could dim them, only allowing enough brightness in to comfort me. I couldn't close the cottage door, but I could enclose my private space. My bed covers ensured my seclusion when I pulled them up over my head. It didn't matter how hot it was during the night, I was not removing the covers.

I was as scared as hell, but I was in my private room; I could ponder, sniff, and pray all night long. I could hide from bears, or I could place myself in whatever world I wanted to be in.

My private room was where I received my justice because no one could see my tears. I could pray like I use to hear Mama pray and the way they prayed in church. I would miss Daddy something awful, and sometimes it seemed like he would visit me and take the fear and trouble back with him.

The dread of bears was my greatest fear; it greatly contributed to my bedwetting and having to lay in it all night. I certainly didn't want to give a bear a reason to run into our barracks and pull me out to kill me, so I hid in my private room. But, if I heard someone flush the toilet, I would get up hurriedly and run to the toilet to relieve myself. Mr. Ellis didn't allow any of the guys to drink water after 8:30 in the evening; I tried to be smart and not drink anything after dinner.

Fear had caused me to become a light sleeper so that any movement in the cottage would wake me. Sometimes when the night watchman, Mr. Capshaw, came into the cottage to clock in, I would wake up. At first, and in my sleepy state, I would think he was a bear; then suddenly, I would have this great urge to pee. By the time I realized it was Mr. Capshaw, I was too afraid to jump up and run to the bathroom.

As soon as I heard him complete the bed check and walk out the door, sometimes it was my sign to run to the bathroom. Once in a great while, though, I was doomed to the wet bed. When that happened, when the 5:30 a.m. bugle sounded, I had to hit the floor, snatch back the covers and strip off the sheets from my bed, run down the hall, deposit the wet sheets in the soiled bin, grab the clean sheets, return to my bed, flip the mattress, and completely make the bed. Then, I had to run to take a quick shower and not be late for formation and the breakfast line, or I would be given a grade.

Sometimes, I could hear another guy call his mom while dreaming, and I understood. I didn't know if it was any of the younger boys, but it didn't matter. We all cried at some point or another because of our fears about bears or tales about the school in general. However, that wasn't an everyday occurrence.

I have always known this fact: when you see someone cry, they're hurt, I mean really hurt. Imagine a young guy working on this slave plantation, paying a debt to society that was an imaginary lie, and then his mother dies in the process. That hurts enough to cry.

Fears of unknown injustice, physical pain, or feeling thrown away or forgotten about, sometimes that was enough to make any of us cry.

These are the remnants of the scary Robinson Cottage of 1957. I took this picture in 2017, sixty years later. It still sits in the woods as it did then, although dilapidated now. Memories will always linger of those times at The Florida School for Boys.

CHAPTER 15
Peonage

*9*n the beginning, I did not know that we were slaves.

The Black side of the FSB aka Dozier campus was just a system of free labor. At the formal end of slavery in the United States, White Southern America was at a loss for free or cheap labor. The FSB plantation was a major production area for fresh produce, processed foods, dairy, fresh meat, animal feed, and more. We were no different than the adult Black men who were falsely arrested or arrested on charges so insignificant that a White man would only be glanced at by the authorities.

Most of the southern states, including Florida, had a shortage of manual labor workers. These states placed laws on the books that only targeted black people. Orlando and surrounding towns were heavily populated with migrant workers known for seasonal work, picking oranges and working on the farms in surrounding towns, picking peas and tomatoes, pulling corn, etc. These workers would be arrested for most anything where the courts saw that they could get a few months of free labor from them.

Mostly Blacks arrived in town by the bus load with migrant farm workers. Men were stopped by the police, questioned, and arrested on minor charges, taken to jail, and charged with something, anything, being that they were out-of-towners. Drinking beer in public, trespassing, vagrancy, or something else minor, and the court would give them a jail sentence for up to a year, or longer if they were charged with an offense while in jail. They were then farmed out to City farms and county laborer road crews, cleaning up the parks, etc., or industries looking for free or cheap labor.

Such was the case at The Florida School for Boys. The Black boys were the "no class," being trained as slaves. A marketable education was not available to us by design. By under educating us, our chances for success were limited and thus returning through the revolving door back into the penal system was almost assured.

The education system at the school for most, if not all, Black boys ended at the third or fourth grade. The only trade we were taught was how to be good slaves on the various farm and vegetable crews, dairy crew, slaughter and processing plants, poultry farms, and kitchen workers, just to name a few.

The word "school" at the Florida School for Boys meant perpetual servitude for the Black boy. The south side, or the White side, of the campus offered attractive housing and a fully functional educational system with training and certifications in the lucrative trades. There was a canteen, a pool, a hospital and dental clinic, a woodworking shop, electrical and mechanic shop, a church, a post office, a laundry, and other buildings and opportunities that supported functional living and educational settings.

Most of the Black boys didn't know what we had done wrong or why we were sent to this modern-day slave plantation. We all came from poor families. Our parents were uneducated or undereducated. They were also lied to and afraid of the White man's justice system, and too poor to hire legal representation.

My brother Art and I were systematically shaped for a charge of truancy. We were constantly being detained in the juvenile system for charges like getting lost and walking through a White neighborhood, only to be charged with "thinking about stealing" or for just having the last name Huntly.

During these many detention center trips, we were unable to attend school and there were no educational opportunities provided to us in the juvenile detention centers. The school where we were registered was not informed of our detention stay or it failed to record this information; therefore, we were labeled as truants. In addition, I was also charged as "incorrigible."

During my stay at FSB, I rarely saw a White boy. They were never assigned to work the fields or in any of the work details where Black boys were assigned. It would be safe to say that while we worked the farms and fields, the White boys were in the classrooms or trade centers. They didn't know the excruciating experiences of working outside in subfreezing conditions or during the extreme heat of summer. They would never have experienced the brutal conditions of working the cane fields in the dead of winter or being subjected to the dangerous conditions in the meat processing plants.

We were paid for our labor once a year, at Christmas. We only worked for a miserable, once a year pay-day. My check for that year was about $7.00 in gifts. Christmas time was a happy time for everyone, especially for most of us who worked outdoors in the cold. Except for the dairy and poultry crews, it was a day off. The guys who were fortunate enough to receive gift boxes from home received them on Christmas day. The rest of us received Christmas bags from the State of Florida on Christmas Day. These bags consisted of a couple of oranges, tangerines, an assortment of nuts, a mini fruitcake, and a box of chocolate covered cherry candy.

Most of us were not able to receive that gift box from home, as our families were indigent and were suffering financial hardships. It didn't bother most of the guys; many of them were just like me. I didn't care if I ever saw a box of cherry candy or a fruit cake ever again. Christmas was always just another day whether we were at home or at FSB. The difference was, when at home everyone usually got tangible gifts; love and togetherness were most important.

At FSB, there were the "haves" and the "have nots." Most of the guys tried to show that it didn't bother them because they had genuine friends and homeboys willing to share their holiday goodies. The more fortunate guys also had money on their accounts (canteen) where they could buy little things to share with the "have nots." I shared with the "have nots," too, when I brought in goodies.

The property of The Florida School for Boys Plantation would be decorated for Christmas, and it was breathtaking—beautiful, absolutely gorgeous on the outside. The Black guys were pressed into service to hang the Christmas lights and set out the lawn decorations. People came from all over Florida to see the decorations at the FSB. I don't believe anyone ever thought about how the young boys lived behind those colorful lights, or how they were being treated. This was a time of segregation; the Black boys' voices didn't seem to matter to the White people. They never got tired, cold or too hot, and we were not human to many.

ඟ

In 1957, I was eleven years old. I'll never forget that winter. We cut and gathered cane like full grown men. After cutting the cane, we made cane juice that later was processed into syrup. Many stalks of cane were given away; I didn't know to who. We loaded the wagon and it would be driven from the field.

We became masters at making cane syrup. We used mule power to operate the cane mill. The mule went around in a circle all day attached to a tong or level. As we took the cane stalks off the trailer, they were fed into a hopper and the stalks would go through the little wheels where it was crushed. We watched as the juice ran into this big drum where it would be cooked. It would turn brown as it continued boiling in that big vat, getting thicker as it turned into syrup.

All of that was interesting, but it wasn't the syrup we were looking for, it was the heat from the vat. It was so cold when we were cutting cane. A wood fire was used to heat up that giant cooking vat. The guy at the mill didn't have to worry about wood because the field crew stockpiled it daily. We were happy to bring the cane to the mill so we could warm our nearly frozen bodies.

I didn't know it was better to allow your hands and feet thaw and warm up without an excessive heat source, including the use of warm water. I had a bad experience trying to warm up from the heat of the fire at the mill. Mr. Stevens often told us not to try to get warm too fast; he'd tell us if we did, it would be pretty painful when the feeling began to come back in our hands and feet. I found out that pain would make a person want to cry. Even if you were a person that did not cry, you were almost guaranteed to do so.

During cane harvesting, we would sharpen up the hoes, our main tools. We even took extra ones to make sure they were sharp and ready to be used effectively. Typically, cane was harvested using a machete, but because of our ages and our detainee status, those tools were considered inappropriate. We took extra files just in case we had to sharpen a hoe in the field. We would all get on this little wagon trailer and the tractor hauled us out to the fields where we would work for the day. That little tractor trailer also hauled the cane to the mill to make syrup.

Cutting cane was a two-man (boy) job. One person would hold the cane and the other person would cut it on the bottom, as close to the root as possible. When chopping cane, we had to be careful of the cane leaves; they were sharp and could slice through your skin as easily as a sharp knife.

One morning, it was bitter cold when we arrived in the cane field; the temperature was in the mid-teens. My feet, hands, ears, and nose had no feeling in them. Icicles had popped up out of the ground. It was beautiful to see how the ice separated the mud and showed itself. It took extra effort to cut the frozen cane stalks; it required all the strength we had.

That unforgettable morning will remain in my mind forever as if it were yesterday. A guy named Jenkins and I were working together as partners that day. One of us would hold back a bunch of cane stalks so the other could chop the cane at the base, and we then loaded it onto the trailer. We took turns. This was a job a grown man could do alone, but men used a machete.

It's was my turn to do the cutting as Jenkins held the bunch of cane. I was chopping at the cane with the hoe. The stalks were frozen solid, and it took several hits to cut them.

Mr. Stevens was yelling out to everybody, "The cane is cold, ya got to hit it hard or y'all gonna be on that one bunch all day! If y'all wanna get to the fire so ya can warm up, ya better get that cane cut! Hurry up, let's go!"

I don't think any of us were able to move fast, everybody was calling for Mr. Stevens' attention. I assumed everybody was having one problem or another.

Mr. Stevens yelled out in a loud voice, "You can't cut the cane like a got-damn wash woman. Hell, put some force behind that damn hoe, it'll cut it!"

The hoes we used were the ones used in the 1930's - 1940's. They were made from heavy metal. We had to drive a wedge in the handle to repair it to prevent the metal parts from spinning around on the handles. The hoes were very heavy to me and I'd been chopping on this bunch of cane for a while. Jenkins was holding the bunch and I was still chopping away at the frozen cane stalks.

Mr. Stevens was still yelling. "You can't play with it, damn-it! You got to hit it, and let's go so we can get warm! Let's go!"

My nose was freezing cold; I couldn't feel it running. My lips barely had feeling in them; they were so cold, I could hardly talk. My ears were freezing and there was no feeling in my hands. I only knew I was holding the hoe and my feet and legs were like a chunk of ice. The only reason I knew they were attached to me was because I was still standing.

This had been a hard, cold morning. The cane we cut was stacked in clusters. I don't know how many stalks of cane were in that cluster, but I had wasted enough time on it. I raised the hoe up as if it were straight toward the heavens and came down with all my might against the frozen cane stalk. I was determined to cut that cane before I got a grade and ended up at The White House.

I brought the hoe down with extra force and somehow it hit one or two stalks of the frozen cane, but most of the force missed the cane and hit the front top of my right boot. The force behind the hoe sliced through my boot as if there was no leather there and cut the top of my big toe off.

My whole body trembled, and for that moment I didn't even know where I was. I tried to gather my senses, realizing something was wrong. I saw the blood. My feet felt frozen. Blood was gushing out of my boot. I realized I was hurt. I shouted, "My foot, my foot!"

Jenkins was calling for Mr. Stevens. I just sat on the frozen ground. Blood was running everywhere. My foot was throbbing and I called out in pain. It seemed like it took forever for help to come. I called out for Daddy. I forgot for a minute he was gone. I was holding steady, but the image on my face displayed the pain in my shaking body as I sat there in the cold. *"Lord, this is Richard! Have mercy! My foot hurts!"* I continued to call out for Mr. Stevens' help.

I didn't know what to do. Then I heard Jenkins say, "He coming, Hunt! He's coming!"

I continued moaning watching the blood gushing from my boot.

Mr. Stevens finally came. He stood back and looked at the situation. From the expression on his face, he appeared frightened by what he saw. He took a deep breath before he spoke. "Can you take your shoe off?

"I don't know, sir," I mumbled.

"Take off the shoe…let's see how bad it is."

All the crew stopped working and gathered around me, asking if I was alright.

Mr. Stevens helped me to get my shoe off. He wrapped my foot in some first aid stuff and helped me get to the wagon. He told me to hold my foot up to slow the bleeding.

While everyone else went back to work, I stayed on the back of that wagon with my foot propped up. Quotas had to be made, and my toe wasn't life threatening. I was scared and didn't know how much damage had been done to my foot. I was concerned—what if I couldn't work the fields anymore? Would I end up like Fred? We never saw him again. What was going to happen to me now? I had never seen a guy get hurt on the job and then taken to the doctor.

My pain tolerance was low and the throbbing in my foot was still present. I was fearful of the unknown. I couldn't call anyone to help me—not my dad, mother, brother, nobody but God. I prayed and asked God to take me away from this place and please let me go home. I was hurt and thrown on the back of the wagon like a bunch of cane stalks.

We rode to the fields every work day in a wagon similar to this one. This is very similar to the wagon I sat on the back of when the top of my toe was severed. We had to have a load of sugar cane before going to the infirmary. Credited to Florida Memory.

Being injured didn't make the cold weather any warmer, but not working and not burning energy made it seem even colder. I could still hear some of the other guys struggling to work the cane, while sniffing their snot as it was running from their noses uncontrollably. There was no feeling in our extremities, and we ached from the hard work and the cold weather ravaging our young bodies. I had cut my foot and didn't know how bad it was, but I lost a great deal of blood. It was so cold; my teeth were chattering. We were freezing, but Mr. Stevens still insisted on meeting his daily quota of cane. I had to dismount the wagon and sit on some cane leaves while the wagon was loaded.

Finally, hours later and just before lunchtime, I was on my way to the infirmary, but only after that load of cane was taken to the cane syrup mill. The other guys were now on the trailer with me and we were all being hauled from the field.

It was above freezing, but still really cold. I had settled down a bit. The throbbing pain had ended, probably because my foot had been elevated, but the sharp pain continued. I was scared to do too much moving around. Once we reached the infirmary, I fought against the stabbing pain. The throbbing returned moments after I lowered my foot to walk. I managed to take short steps, walking on the heel of my right foot. Mr. Stevens walked with me inside the building and explained to the doctor how my accident happened.

Immediately, the medical staff started to patch me up. When my foot was unwrapped, it was ugly, and it started to really ache again something awful.

I didn't know if the medical staff were doctors or nurses, and they didn't seem to have any mercy for this little Black guy. They tugged at the severed skin and dabbed a swab of cotton that had been soaked with a brown, burning solution against the reminder of my toe. This was more painful than the injury. "OUCH, OUCH!" I yelled. I panted through the treatment. I was told by the person working on my foot, "Okay, you can hush, you gon' be alright so hush now. Shut up!"

At no time do I remember being given any medication to numb the pain. Even more insensitive were the series of questions accusing me of deliberately hurting myself to get out of work.

"You didn't mean to do this much damage to yourself, did you?" the doctor said.

Fear of the thought of what he was trying to say to set me up for a trip to The White House to be beaten was more powerful than the throbbing pain in my foot. "No sir! I mean . . . I didn't do this on purpose," I answered. "It was an accident!" That was a double dose of a heavy burden. I couldn't hold back my tears this time. My lips were clenched while the tears silently crawled down to my chin.

"Well . . . you really did it to yourself," the doctor said. "You will have to stay out of work for a while . . . a few weeks anyway."

I asked, "Will I be going back to my crew?"

He said, "No! I don't think so. I'm sending you over to the school and they can figure out what to do with you."

My mind raced with uncertainty. What was next for me? What will happen if I can't work? The thought was really frightening. I realized they thought I had intentionally hurt myself. Mr. Stevens was right there, and he told them what happened.

One of the guys, a Black guy, who worked at the infirmary asked, "What you scared about, man?"

"They think I hurt myself on purpose." Then I had a question for him: "What are they talking about doing? Are they trying to send me to The White House now?" I asked.

"Naw, man. They just trying to scare you."

"You mean, they're gonna send me home?"

"Hell, naw!" he said while laughing.

"What happens in times like this and what're they talking about doing with me, man?"

"Right now, you gone get some crutches and walk your ass right up outta here to that school over there," he said, and he was right.

I struggled getting back to the school alone. It was a long walk because the crutches and I didn't get along too well at first.

CHAPTER 16
The Processing Plant

*7*he processing plant was another world altogether. While the other guys from my cottage went to work in the field, I had to spend every day at school. I don't remember how many days passed when I requested to speak to Mr. Mitchell. I told him I was ready to go back to work and if he let me go back, I promised I would stay out of everybody's way. Although I was still noticeably limping, I also promised him I would keep up and not slow the crew down.

Mr. Mitchell returned me to the field crew, and I worked as hard as I could. I never got used to the crutches, so I just put them aside as often as I could. By the time I was completely healed, I was transferred to the processing plant.

We were told to do a job and that was what we did, or we risked being beaten half to death. There was no doubt in my mind if you had to choose between slaughtering animals and taking a ride to the White House, you would choose to work the slaughter job.

Every day I went to work, we butchered animals. The farm dairy crews would bring in the livestock for us to kill. My moto was, just leave them in a stall, we'll take it from there. Cows, hogs, chickens, turkeys—you name it, we killed it. Before I stepped inside of a slaughterhouse, I was a meat lover. That was before I saw what really happened behind those doors. Animals that were crippled, blind, hurt, and perhaps even diseased all went down the same slaughter chutes. Sudden death awaited them at the end. It was possible that an animal or parts of it could be the main course on somebody's table the same day.

My first job was as the Slaughter Pin Master. I didn't realize at first that the job was up for grabs and no one else wanted it. Along with my transition from the fields came this job; I had to take it. Make no mistake about what I say: at my station, boys, weaklings, and the fainthearted were not welcome. My whole existence depended on having the courage and determination to get in the pen with those animals and force them into the chute for slaughter. I had to actually be in the open with those big cows and hogs.

Most of them were several times my weight. Each animal slaughtered was raised with an electric winch attached to a scale that determined their weight, which was close to half a ton and sometimes greater. Here I was, looking at some of them eye to eye. I wondered what they were thinking, knowing at the end of that day my face would be the last thing they remember.

No one would understand how hard it was to force a hog to go in a direction it didn't want to go. I wrestled with cows and hogs trying to push them into a chute to die. Sometimes the animals raised terrible commotion. Many times, my heart was in my hand, not in my chest. I was terrified.

When looking into the faces of the animals, I just knew one or more of them could charge and ram little ole me against the wall at any time, or I could get knocked down. There would be so many animals in the pen, no one would be able rescue me before I was seriously injured or trampled to death.

I prayed each time I had to get in the pen with those cows and hogs. *Lord, it's Richard again, I know you're busy and I know I call on you constantly for help because I know you'll bring me through safely. Thanks for answering me.*

I believed the animals knew their death was imminent. They knew I could have suffered permanent injury, as had happened to others before me. I often wondered who was going to give a true report of a twelve year old Black boy who had been placed in that kind of danger.

Being knocked down by the cows and hogs so regularly had become normal. Jumping to my feet as quickly as possible was the key to remaining alive, and taking a bath in animal feces, blood, urine, and mud came with the territory. Hogs, cows, and bulls just tossed me around in the mud and muck all the time. It didn't matter that we had "hot shots" (long battery operated poles that had two forks or prongs on the end to shoot a bolt of electricity into the animal) to help get the stubborn animals into the slaughter chute or back the animal up enough for me to get out of the way.

The animal in the chute would be guided into a position to be shot. For a second it would be quiet. The man would look the animal in the face and point the sawed off twenty-two rifle at its head, but sometimes, the animal would suddenly move just as he was about to pull the trigger. POP! He'd miss his target!

Imagine an animal the size of a cow or bull being shot, but not killed? That animal then becomes a killer. He would be outraged and attack anything in its way with killer force.

I saw it happen. If there was a cow, and the chute that held him was made of wood, that cow was powerful enough to burst through the door that was blocked off.

The man with the gun would have to shoot the animal until it was brought down. POP! POP! POP! He'd have to reload between each shot. That kind of killing was not a pretty sight to see. That moment, if I was in the wrong position, I could have also been an instant fatality.

I was also aware of the things that could go wrong. The hogs would be lined up inside the chute. The hog that was up front, and next to be killed, would try to back up. I couldn't let him turn around, so I'd run to the back of the chute, from the outside, and punch him with the hot shot. Then he'd try to run forward. I knew the animals could sense death, that's why they would try so desperately to escape.

The gun man would be standing at the front of that chute, just waiting for the animal to finally turn his head to face him. All he needed was that one second, and POP! He'd shoot the animal right between the eyes.

Instantly, the squealing stopped, and the kicking and trembling starts. The animal would drop to the floor. The man with the gun would snatch the board from in front of the chute while someone else put another board behind him so the next animal stayed in place.

⟳

Not too long after my twelfth birthday, I was transferred to Bunche Cottage. I believed my brother Arthur had lived in Bunche Cottage. He had been released now, and the school moved me in since he left. I was happy for Art. He made it out. Except for that short period after Daddy died, I really didn't get to know Deno. It seemed the guys at Dozier knew his reputation better than I did. Art was the good guy. He stayed out of trouble and was well-liked. I guess that's why he made Ace rank and earned an early release.

Poor me, we arrived at Dozier at the same time and I could never get out of the Grub rank it seemed. I prayed I wouldn't have to prove myself again. But everywhere I went, if nobody heard of me, then I had to re-establish myself. However, most of the guys at Bunche had heard about me before I got there. We carried our own weight wherever we went. Art didn't like to fight; he had a special knack for talking his way out of a confrontation. My talk wasn't so good, and I paid for it time after time.

I continued to work at the slaughterhouse processing plant after my transfer to Bunche Cottage. I learned all aspects of working at the plant. The next job this twelve year old was introduced to was that of a minor butcher. Every day I learned more and more about how to slaughter animals. My job was to prepare the meat from the fresh kill for the master butchers to cut up. Meat was processed for the Black and White sides of campus, as well as for sale off of the state property.

The tools were carefully cared for; knives were kept as sharp as a razor. There was a tool called "the sharpening steel" that was used to sharpen our knives when needed. We used steel gloves, a must to protect our hands from those razor sharp knives.

We had zero job training, meaning we watched what other guys were doing and we did the same. Danger circled us like a web, so always remaining focused was critical.

Looking back, it makes me wonder how I made it through. I didn't realize I was being placed in harm's way. Death could have come suddenly at a moment's notice. Thank God for bringing me through; He never stops protecting my life.

Most of the time I worked with hog slaughtering. After the hog was killed, part of my job was to grab the hind leg and another person grabbed the front and we would spin it around. Then one of us would take a long sharp knife and slice into the throat of the animal. Blood would spew out like turning on a faucet. I would slit the hind legs so we could hook the leaders with a steel hook on the winch and jack the animal up to let the blood drain from it. One of us used the water hose to wash the blood into the drain. This procedure was repeated, one hog after another, until all the hogs in the pen had been slaughtered for that day.

Scraping the hair off the hog was next. The winch would move the hog down the line to a boiler where scalding hot water was poured on it for several minutes to thin the hair on their body. Then it was time for us to scrape the hair down to their bare skin. That hog was rinsed again and readied for the master butcher who would slit it straight down the center of the stomach to the head. We used a container to catch the intestines of the hogs as they rolled out. We separated the liver and the heart; those were put in different containers.

All the "chitlins" (chitterlings) were made from the intestines of the hog. Some of the trailer guys were assigned to this detail. This was where hours were spent using their hands to strip all the intestinal lining, and just like working the fields, they didn't have protective gloves. They were required to clean the intestines all day, every day. They had to squeeze all the food particles and feces out of the intestines.

A few months later I scalded my right foot at the boiler water area. Somebody else had worn the protective rubber boots that I had been wearing and I had to start work without them. There was no one, not even the crew leader, who would listen to my complaint or who would help me get a pair of boots. There were a set number of boots in the supply corner for the guys that worked the slaughterhouse on the even day crew and the odd day crew. For some reason one pair of boots were busted. If I had taken time to find another boot, I would've been late for work and I would've received a grade. I had come out of the Grub with zero write ups and didn't want to go back; the Grubs meant 98% of every grade was a beating, and that's taking a chance with your life. I took my chances working with a busted boot. That was a mistake!

The boiling hot water poured down onto my shoe and soaked through to my foot. Instantly, I did an African dance.

I didn't recognize myself. I couldn't get that boot off of my foot quick enough, using my left foot to push my right boot off. A fire bolt of heat shot from my foot and attacked all of my nerves and sent shock waves throughout my entire body. My heart pounded like it was on overload. There was a fire in my bones, and nobody was able to put it out. Every bone in my body felt that pain. As a matter of fact, the pain produced from The White House beatings couldn't match the pain of being scalded with boiling hot water. Next came that prayer I had never prayed before, "Lord, why me?"

Somehow, someway, I was taken to the infirmary. I don't remember much more except a cooling feeling. I remember laying on an examination table and my foot was in a bucket of cool liquid. The nurse was pouring more cool liquid into the bucket from a large bottle. I could feel myself breathing. The cool solution felt like it was crawling up my leg; the pain was easing; the fire in my foot and bones was going out. I felt relief from the intense burning pain. The cool liquid had stopped the burning in the same foot as my half-severed toe. I wondered, *Lord, what's next?*

"Whatcha gon' do to yourself next time, boy?" The doctor said. He was the same doctor that worked on my toe months earlier. He said, "Seem like you keep trying to get out of work boy. Don't worry, I'm going to get this fixed up. I'll have your little Black ass back to work in a short while. Every time I look around some of y'all are trying to get out of work. I'll just fix you up and put you right back out there. You will be able to go back to work in no time."

The nurse approached with two hypodermic needles and gave me two shots.

The doctor stood up. "Keep your foot in that solution for a while, and then I'll get it cleaned up and bandaged. You got a second degree burn on your foot." I didn't care what degree burn I had. I didn't know what the doctor was talking about because a burn was a burn to me, and it hurt like hell.

The nurse finished applying some white cream to my foot. He used gauze pads and rolled gauze around my foot to apply the bandage. Finally, she secured all the gauze with bandage tape. I don't know what was in that cream, but I was now only having minor pain.

I was given a pair of crutches and a note for my cottage father to allow me to return to the infirmary twice a week, Monday's and Wednesdays or Tuesdays and Thursdays. The infirmary had the office boy walk me back to the cottage. I promised myself this time I would learn to use the crutches.

We weren't allowed to keep pain medicine in the lockers, the cottage father had to keep that. If we had pain, he would give us medicine for what ills we had.

‐‐‐‐‐‐‐‐‐ ໙ ‐‐‐‐‐‐‐‐‐

We raised prize-winning animals on that plantation. When their glory days were over, I would meet them at the processing plant to be slaughtered.

Make no mistake about it, a hog or pig is used from the "rudi to the tudi", from pig ears to pig heels. I mean everything was processed, from intestines to cooking oil (lard). Even the hog's genitals were used as a delicacy called mountain oysters.

What a traumatic life we lived. Damn! No matter how much I would wash off, the scent of blood stayed in my skin, clothes, shoes, face, and hair. We were furnished rubber boots to wear, and they would be filled with blood by the time the slaughtering was over for the day.

We also slaughtered chickens; a day killing chickens was also a day to remember. The chickens came in cages with so many to each cage. Chickens were processed a little differently. They were hung up on a rack, several of them at a time.

As soon as the chickens were taken out of the cages, they began begging for their lives. It was almost like they were saying, "Please! Please! Please!" They would peck you while you were trying to hang them up; that hurt, too.

One of my jobs was to use an electric knife and go down the line cutting their throats. While their blood dripped all over me and the floor, the chickens did a lot of wing flapping. When that stopped, they were ready for the hot water tank. Next, they were passed through a machine that picked most of the feathers off their carcasses. However, the feathers that were left on the chickens, you guessed it, we had to pick off manually.

After all the feathers were removed, the chickens were unclamped and put on the table. Our next job was to remove their insides. We split them right under their tail between the legs. Then we stuck our hand inside of the chicken and brought his whole insides out quickly. We cut the feet off. The feet and intestines were thrown into a container and dumped into the tank to be cooked and fed to the hogs. Folks from the country, the Deep South, knew what that was all about, but the city people would have to brace for that kind of action.

The doctor had ordered 'light duty' after my scalding until my foot was completely healed. There were only two jobs at the processing plant that qualified as light duty, cleaning hog intestines and gutting chickens. I was given a tall stool to pull up to the table while the other guys had to stand. Each day I was told where to place my stool, and each morning before I left the cottage, I prayed my job for the day would be cutting up chickens, and not clean feces from hog intestines, for the obvious reasons.

Lord, this is Richard here again. Please make my day a safe one for me. I know you can do it.

Thank You, Sir.

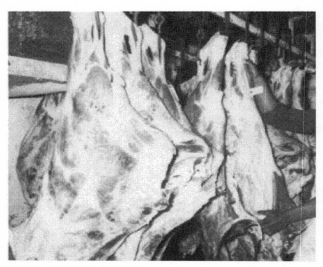

1950's Fresh butchered cows and hogs hanging there waiting for the master butchers. Part of my job was to get them right here, the cooler. Credited to: Florida Memory.

CHAPTER 17
Arthur

*G*od blessed my brother Arthur. He and I were sent to the school together, but due to good behavior he was released within our first year.

Art told me when he was sent home, our mother was very happy to see him, but she had sent two boys off to be educated, and only one returned. When Art returned home, he filled Mama in on the details of The Florida School for Boys. He told her only enough to put her into action. He didn't tell her everything because he didn't want her to worry about anything, she was powerless to change.

Mama had one of her friends write a letter to Superintendent Mitchell inquiring about me. Mr. Mitchell sent her a return letter. When Art returned to the plantation, he told me about the letters. At the time, I didn't hear anything he said. I was so overwhelmed that Mama cared about me. I was elated, I had a constant smile. My mind sang out these few words, "Damn, Mama does care about me!"

When I returned home in October 1958, Mama let me see that letter from the school. It read something like this:

Dear Mrs. Huntley,
The school received your letter concerning your son, Richard Huntly. He is doing fine now. We just don't know

what came over him. He's been having a little bit of a problem following the rules. It appears as though Richard is having a rough time accepting his brother was able to abide by the rules and go home early.

Richard got into a little trouble the other day and we had to give him a little spanking as a punishment. The supervisor that wrote him up said several times he had to warn him about fighting and talking out of turn. He recommended him for a spanking, but he's doing fine now, and if he can stay out of trouble for the next few months, he will be able to go home, too. Thank you for writing us and you may write us any time. We will be happy to give you a report on him.

Thank you.
Mr. Mitchell
School Superintendent.

Once home, Art slipped up and was sent back. I couldn't talk with him right away, but I felt bad for him. This time he was put on the dairy crew. He had to get up in the morning by 3:30 am, dress, go out to round up cows, and milk them. Then he had to get back to the cottage in time to eat breakfast along with everybody else, and then hit the field again. They allowed him only to go to school for half days. It didn't matter the weather, rain or shine, hot or cold, and sometimes in the sleet or snow. When I did get a chance to see him, he had tears in his eyes.

He said, "Bro, they beat me because one of the cows was in the wrong stall. They said I was supposed to know every one of a hundred or more cows by the color of their face and I didn't. I didn't know how the face supposed to look."

I asked, "Do you know now?"

"I think I do, Bro." Then, the last thing he told me, "Bro, they made me stay with a cow all night while the cow gave birth to her calf. If anything went wrong when the cow was having the calf, I had to pull the calf out of the cow. And if the calf died or something bad happened, that would be a write up. I would have to ride to The White House for it."

On behalf of my brother, I was mad. The expression on my face clearly stated that. I told my brother, "This is a place for a man. Nobody has pity for a crying man. Crying is for little children. Bro, there are no crybabies at this place. I can't help you man. My hands are tied, Bro. Be strong, you won't be here that long, and you'll be going back home."

It wasn't often Art came to me and I couldn't help him. That talk let me know I couldn't be there for my brother at all times. But he knew when at all possible, I would be right there.

CHAPTER 18
Bunche Cottage

I learned to follow the rules and prayed I would never visit The White House again. I was well past my twelfth birthday and I had outgrown the smaller cottage. Through some formula, the higher-ups believed I had progressed or matured enough to handle the more difficult situation I would be faced with; hence, I spent my remaining time at the Dozier plantation assigned to Bunche Cottage. My foot was still bandaged, and I was continuing to receive treatment.

With each transfer to a higher-level cottage came a higher level of trouble. An altercation with another guy in the new cottage almost got me a ride straight to the White House. The new cottage father heard the loud noises and rushed to break up the ruckus. I insisted on having the last word with the other guy and continued running my mouth.

The cottage father grabbed me by the back of my shirt. "I don't like your attitude, so shut the hell up or I'll have The Blue Goose pick you up right now!" he yelled out.

I froze. "Yes, sir."

"Get your little ass to the end of the basketball court and sit there!"

Again, I said, "Yes, sir." I prayed he didn't call for back up, meaning that Blue Goose. I didn't know how it would've played out if I got a write-up for talking back to the cottage father. That would have been worse than running away. But I may as well have gotten that beating, because I didn't see what was coming next.

Now that I was in another cottage, walking a straight line was difficult. I just couldn't get it right. I asked myself if I was crazy. A couple of days later, two other guys and I were walking from work in the evening, heading to the cottage. We cut across the grass in front of the school. We were just talking about nothing really. Suddenly, we heard a loud voice yelling, "What the hell y'all walking on my damn grass for? Come here, all of you! Huntly, you've been here over a year. I know you knew better."

That report went to my cottage father and for some reason I had a bad feeling. I believed I was already on his bad side; thinking back, I might have gotten a grade for that little argument. Anyway, the cottage father recommended an attitude adjustment for me, meaning a trip to the torture chamber for a beating.

Lord have mercy, my trouble started from a simple argument with one of the guys. I believed I was only scolded that time, but it caused the cottage father to have a negative impression about me, and that caused me to have a repeat of the same old near-death experience. One never knew the end results of a beating until it was over. This trip proved to be much different from the other times I took that ride. This time it was like stepping into a fire in The White House. I was scared to death.

Lord, please hear my prayer. This is Richard. Let me live.

It seemed like they did one of the other boys worse when he started screaming and hollering. He got slabbed (flesh literally torn from the bone). It was nasty, and he was hollering for life or death. I didn't know his skin was split open like that until we got out of the car. God knows, it wasn't pretty. He was a mess behind, a big wet spot in the seat of his pants made gnats attack him like he was something good to eat.

I got a beating for just walking on the grass. Hell! As much as I tried, I couldn't keep my nose clean.

I had been out of the Grub for almost two months when my foot got scalded, then I was moved up to Bunche Cottage and I got a grade that first day. I had been feeling kind of proud of myself for not having any run-ins since my first trip to the White House a few months earlier. Most guys worked hard at making rank. I just wanted to survive, get out of the Grub, and not return to the White House. That didn't work out. It was hard to believe, while I was still limping on my scalded foot, then I was beaten for walking on the grass.

It was at least two or three months before I could get back into the pen with the cows and hogs. The doctors wanted to be sure I could move quickly on my foot. I was still ordered to return to the infirmary to have the bandage on my scaled foot changed. I never once believed the staff cared about my foot, but they needed more help in the slaughterhouse preparing the hogs' carcasses for the master butchers. Any of the frailer guys could pull guts out of dead chickens or clean shit from hog intestines. My bandages were changed, and after an examination of my foot I was given another week to clean shit.

᱿

A few weeks later, after my medical treatment, the office boy walked me back to school. Once I entered the building, he turned and hurried back to the infirmary. I had missed my morning water break because I was at the clinic. It was a 90° day, not a day for walking. I was sweating and could've drank a gallon of water. Upon entering the building, there was the water fountain. I didn't see anybody and I went for it. After three or four gulps of water, I saw the hem of a dress through my peripheral vision. I looked up slowly, swallowed, and Mrs. Mobley's malicious eyes were staring down at me. She was Mr. Mobley's plain looking wife. She was a brown skinned, tall, slender woman with shoulder length black hair. There was a gap so wide in her upper front teeth, it looked like she was missing a tooth.

"What you doing, boy?" she asked.

Damn, I thought, *she can see what I'm doing*. "I … I … I … was taking a drink of water before I got to class, Mrs. Mobley."

"Where do you belong?" she asked.

I stood staring at Mrs. Mobley and pointing to my classroom.

"Well you're late. Git there!" she said.

My classroom door was open, I walked in and placed the infirmary note on Mr. Evans' desk, While on the way to my seat, I looked back at the door. Mrs. Mobley was standing there talking to Mr. Evans.

By the end of the school day my name was on the write up list. Mr. Evans called me to the front of the class and told me to step outside. I thought for sure I had messed up again and had been recommended to the White House for a beating, and I was. This would be my third trip and only weeks since the last time.

I found out I got written up for drinking water without permission, and out of fear, I had stared up at Mrs. Mobley. There had been a new rule put in place at the school after an unsupervised boy ran away. After that attempt, any boy caught out of class without a proper excuse, or pass, could be given a grade for an attempt to escape if the teacher wished to do so. In addition to a grade for drinking water and staring up at Mrs. Mobley, I was written up for not having a pass even though I was returning from the doctor and had placed the note on Mr. Evans' desk.

I was still in the Grubs when I got these three grades. DAMN! That put me on top of the wanted list. The next school day, when the office boy came to our classroom, I had an idea my name was on the list. I tried to explain to Mr. Evans that I did have a pass and I had put it on his desk. He said he didn't see it. There was no way I could contradict him without risking another write-up or grade for talking back. If I thought I could get away, I sure as hell would've run for the hills. But that was a dangerous game, too. This would be my third ride to the White House. I turned and said my favorite prayer.

Hello Lord, it's me again, Richard. I need your help please. They seem as though they are trying to kill me. Please don't let my life be lost at this place. My body is getting weak from so many beatings. Please, help me, and give me enough strength to hold the bed. Please don't let me be slabbed. Thank you, Lord, again, you never fail me.
Amen.

When we arrived at the White House, Mr. Mobley did his usual thing, he got out of the car and opened the door for us. Mr. Mitchell opened the door to the White House, stepped in, and beckoned for us to step inside. As always, he pointed to the dreadful little room I had sat in twice already, the sight of it made me tremble in my tracks. "Alright . . . y'all know what to do," he said.

In my mind, I was psyching myself up as much as I could, but there was no getting ready for what was about to happen. At The White House, that little squeaky door sound went clean through me. It sounded like a door out of a horror movie scene, except this scene was real; lives had been taken inside of this place and never accounted for.

"Be seated, in that room," Mr. Mobley said.

Next came that little damn speech Mr. Mitchell always gave; I could hear it all in my sleep. The speech is trying to make us feel we were the cause of being there and this was to help us to be better slaves. Only fools believe that.

I didn't know the other guy who rode with me, and I didn't know what to expect. This time, I had three charges. There were only two of us, but it was possible there were more guys waiting to come over, and just too many to drive over at once.

After Mr. Mitchell gave his famous speech about why we were there and how much this was going to hurt him, he had the other guy go into the beating room first, which gave me time to get geared up for what was about to happened to me again. The other guy was shaking all over. The fan was switched on, woo-woo-woo-woo. "You, less go, get on that bed!"

His first lick came; it was a loud muffled sound, like a BOOM, like a sound made from a clap of the hollow palms of a hand. I didn't hear anything from the boy. Boom! I heard a little sniffing, and a third lick and fourth, the guy began to let lose, every lick seemed louder and louder. He began to call for help and calling his parents as well. "God save me!" he cried. It was burning, he couldn't breathe. By this time, he had coughed up spit mixed with tears, snot and sweat. I don't know if he had ridden before, but he was letting me know he knew how to pray just like everybody that came through here. His action was no different than all the rest.

The most devastating part of that beating is the first time. Many of the guys don't make it through. When your flesh is being beat upon until it splits open, the pain is very intense; it's something beyond explanation, and it can't be easily matched.

It seemed to me like his beating was rather short, less than twenty licks and his praying to Jesus ceased. After the first trip to the torture chamber, a repeat beating would drive you insane if you didn't psych yourself up to deal with the pain.

Finally, it was my turn. I was trembling, maybe not visibly, but I knew what was about to happen and the waiting was killing me. I was ready to get it over with. Suddenly, I heard Mr. Mitchell say, "Okay, Huntly. You know what to do!"

Mr. Mobley mumbled under his breath as I took those little fifteen or so steps to get to where he was standing. The strop was behind his back. I already knew what was about to happen and how. The scariest thing about it was I never knew if I would leave there the way I came, alive. *All of this for a drink of water*, I thought.

As I approached the bed, the guy who just got up had already wet the pillow. I could see the fresh snot and tears on the slick shiny wet pillow left for me to explore again. I knew this same pillow had been used by hundreds of others. But that wasn't my worry right then; it didn't matter now, and I laid my head right into that pillow. Suddenly my thoughts were interrupted by that killer blow to my backside.

My brain could never prepare for that pain. BOOM! I moaned in a loud grunt. My brain was going insane as I tried to brace myself for the next blow to my body. BOOM! My mind was on fire. BOOM! I held on tight and waited for the next blow. BOOM! I believed to my soul, the pain I was suffering now woke up one of my ancestors who may have died from being in shock from the beating he received. Would the same thing happen to me? BOOM!

The heavy blows seemed to be getting lighter. It seemed like I heard voices saying, "You'll make it; you'll survive and never forget." It seemed like with every blow from that point, I let out a groan into that snot and tear-stained pillow. I left my portion of tears in it also. My body also drifted away, somewhere in between the pressure of holding the bed and hollering out into empty space. I was panting, sweating, and breathing hard in short bursts and moaning through my nose, while holding the pain inside my gut. I assumed I lost consciousness or maybe one of my ancestors visited and took some of the pain for me, saying, *"Don't die. Hold on, don't come here yet, go back and tell the world how this pain felt to Black men—us as slaves owned by a Massa, beat to death with no mercy."*

It seemed as if the pain became somewhat bearable. I heard Mr. Mobley's feet scratch the floor just before he hit me with a powerful blow. In my mind, I left my body there until I heard Mr. Mobley say, "Get up!" Then I returned to my body.

When I got up from the bed, it felt like I weighed an extra fifty pounds. I knew my flesh had been temporally torn away from the bones in my butt and legs and had to be mentally repaired instantly so I could walk. I was weak and stumbled for a second, but quickly gained my consciousness and reprogrammed my awareness to connect with reality. I knew I had died and come back to life. I have suffered pain my ancestors could never explain, no human can explain the pain I endured of being beaten so ruthlessly; no, not even me.

I was returned to my cottage after dinner with the only energy I had left. I had to walk as normally as I could and my little chest stuck out. That took every bit of strength I could find, signaling that I survived. Once a guy was returned from the White House whole, he was recognized as a hard dude, and was respected for his endurance. Nobody handed him any shit because his home boys would tear their asses up. I had to walk slow and take my time to regain full potential. I still had a limp from the previous injury to my foot; that meant double trouble with walking, showering, sitting, and sleeping at night.

It was during these times when I learned to laugh, talk, joke, play games and act normal. At the same time, my heart would be full of so much pain and sorrow. I cried out for mercy within the walls of my little chest, not to be seen, but in my mind. I asked the question, *Lord, why so much suffering?*

We didn't spend much time at the cottage, but it operated by a similar system. Behind those walls was just as deadly as any part of the school. All of the staff were there to keep us educationally ignorant, to break our spirits, and train us to be submissive slaves in order to keep their jobs. They had to keep "Florida's best kept secret" and keep the profits coming in.

They would take privileges away from us if somebody took off. We were aware of this in Robinson Cottage, but maybe one or two really tried to run away. We were only ten and eleven years old.

Going to another cottage with devils, comes a devil catcher (for every bully, there is a bigger bully to put him down). Each time we were transferred to another cottage, came a higher level of rules. The higher-ups placed the blame of an attempted escape on the head of every cottage member. If a guy was trying to leave at night, the cottage father believed someone in the cottage knew he was trying to run and they expected them to shift (snitch). Not so. No one would ever shift. The guys would nearly kill someone who was a shift.

However, there was another rule that the cottage father expected to be enforced. Not only were the guys rated on a behavioral scale, the cottages were graded by points. If a cottage was scheduled to go to the movie or have a banquet, and somebody tried to escape, your cottage would lose all its points, and had to start all over again with the point system. It was possible the cottage might never get another chance to re-earn the merit points, or it could take as long as a year.

If a guy left at night, he would have a pretty good lead, or jump, before daylight. He'd probably think if he could get far enough away his trail would be lost. That just didn't seem to work out too well, especially for Black boys. In a few hours, they would be back in a sad and pitiful condition.

The runaway would be taken to the White House and beaten continuously with a manmade leather strop about two inches thick by four and a half inches wide, and two and a half feet long. That was their punishment tool. The strop had chips of metal embedded in it, and a hole the size of a silver dollar near its end that would suck up plugs of skin. This strop was designed so each lick did the most damage. It resembles a barber shop razor sharpening belt with the handle. They would beat the boy until his butt was pure mush, splitting him open from his behind down through the back of his thighs. By the time he was returned to his cottage, blood and water, probably urine, soaked his pants and would cover the back of his legs. During the hot summer months, flies and gnats swarmed around his pants feeding off the blood.

When a runaway was captured, Mr. Mitchell and Mr. Mobley would bring him back to the cottage, most of the time around or after dinner, when all the guys were around to see the condition of a captured boy. Sometimes he was possibly raped by the Dog Boys who caught him before he was picked up by the superintendent and his overseer.

They knew the boys in that cottage usually would beat him again after he had already been beaten at the White House. Not everybody was in favor of that kind of treatment because it was cold blooded. But there were boys that feared the White House themselves and would beat the runner while the cottage father looked on.

Sometimes a runner never came back or was just missing the next morning. We'd ask the cottage father, his whereabouts, and did they find him? He would always say their parents came and got them during the night. We never believed their parents would come in the middle of the night.

We were slaves, but we weren't stupid. Either the runner got away, which was unlikely, or most likely he was dead.

As soon as I arrived at Bunche Cottage, I was told about the Dog Boys. These were honor prisoners from the nearby prison in Chipley, Florida, who trained dogs to track escapees from the prison and runners from Dozier.

I never knew about the Dog Boys when I was at Robinson Cottage, probably because the younger boys seldom tried to run. When a younger guy ran, they seldom got off the campus. Hell, most of these guys had to be escorted to another nearby building on campus because they could easily get lost. The guys in Bunch cottage were more mature, worldly, and older, so being tracked down by dogs was another effective deterrent against running. The Dog Boys would also beat the runner for making them run through the woods at night to catch them.

1950's A "Dog Boy" (Prison inmate) with dogs and their owners and trainers. Credited to: Florida Memories, Florida Archives, Tallahassee Florida.

It happened to one of the boys in Bunche Cottage. I don't remember his name, but he said he was caught by the Dog Boys and their dogs. He said if the supervisor hadn't been right there when he got caught, he would've had a problem. The Dog Boys were known to roll the dog, Old Blue, onto his back, and make you kiss his penis, or they'd raise Old Blue's tail and make you kiss the dog's ass. If the dog was a she, her vagina was kissed. Then, if you were a large enough guy, they'd make you pick up the dog and carry him/her back to the truck.

I witnessed the outcome of a merciless beating. It was the punishment of a runaway boy from Bunche Cottage. He took off from the school. This guy was in bad shape when they returned him to our cottage. He was trembling like I had never seen before. I believe he was in shock.

The boy had been 'slabbed,' (beat with the side of the strop) which was not uncommon for that violation. Once they got him to the torture chamber, his life was in their hands. That beating, where his skin was split open, was meant to control his mind and bring harm to his body. They slabbed him intentionally, and his clothes stuck to his open wounds. He had gnats literally clinging to his backside.

When they brought him back to the cottage, he couldn't step out of the car; he had to crawl out. Mr. Mitchell and Mr. Mobley stood and watched him like he was a slimy creature. Then Mr. Mitchell yelled out, "Some niggers gotta learn the hard way!" He stood looking down at him with his hand on his hip. After the guy crawled far enough from the car, they left.

When I saw the wounds on this guy, the way they tortured him, I wouldn't want to go through that kind of torture. I would rather die. Hell! I wanted to die when they beat me three months earlier for drinking water. I guess the Lord had work for me to do. Maybe that's why he kept me above the ground that long.

Naturally, there was a moment of silence, but when we saw how brutally beaten that boy was, it was hard to look at him. Until I actually saw someone whose flesh was ripped and torn like that, I could never understand the depth of what that looked like. They brought him back like he was an example of what would happen to a runaway.

Hell, it bothered me the way they did it. I felt bad for him. At twelve years old, seeing the condition of that guy was painful. My young mind just couldn't process what was happening. When we were with Daddy, we never saw White people do that to one of us. To further confuse me, big Black Mobley did that to him. I had never seen a sight like that before, and that was what it was designed for, to instill fear in us.

When we helped him down to the court, he couldn't sit down. His backside was soaked with blood. He stood there in one spot, trembling. His punishment was too severe for a living soul. He was suffering in pain and too scared to say anything. He had a damn good reason not to. He knew what the consequences of his offence were. He caused the cottage to lose their spot in line for the banquet. It was our time to get a special treatment and a fine meal of fried chicken, ice cream, cake, then go to the movie theater off campus. When somebody took off as a runaway, that messed up everybody else. Some of guys in Bunche Cottage were pretty upset and were ready to kick him to sleep on top of that beating. This was the time when he needed a friend.

The cottage father stood at the end of the court waiting to see the next step of his punishment. The guy was weak; he was just trembling and could hardly stand. There were still one or two guys who wanted to beat him. The cottage father just turned and walked away, shaking his head like he was disappointed.

After a while, this boy—I'll call him Aaron—finally made his way up the steps of the building so he could take a shower before everybody else came in for the night. When he finished and put his shorts on, they stuck to the places that were busted open on his backside. He could barely move. The only medical treatment he received was from flying gnats swarming him and getting drunk from the tainted blood that soaked his busted open pants. No medical treatment administered at all, that was part of the punishment.

Aaron was scared, and it was unusual not to get jumped on, but that day, due to the severe beating, he was spared. Some of the other guys had something to say about that. As time passed, he wouldn't talk about what happened out in those woods after he was caught. When he was asked if the prisoners that caught him did anything to him, he never answered. He would stop smiling and just walk away. Only a smart-ass dummy would even ask that question.

Raping the guys, making them raise the dog's tail and kiss their ass, kissing the dog's penis or making him carry that Old Blue to the truck. I know something happened to Aaron. He was never right after that. When I left FSB, I never saw him again.

It had been at least three months since my last beating. I was still getting in trouble, but the cottage father, Mr. Crockett, would rather maul our heads than give us a grade. Somehow, he kept a record of our offenses in his head. He would take the second joint of his pointer finger and dig it in into our foreheads in a screwing motion, always leaving a whelp and slight bruise. I always thought to myself, no grade, no beating. His punishment was a moment of pain, rather than a grade, loss in rank, or a trip to the White House.

I had just arrived back at the cottage on a cool fall afternoon, tired as I could be. I needed to get cleaned up for dinner. I don't remember what I was thinking about, but it certainly wasn't what I was about to hear when one of my homeboys came. "Hey, Hunt!" he yelled out, "You're going home!" He continued yelling, "You're going home. Woop! Woop! Hunt is going home!"

Right away, I took his comments for a joke and I returned it with one saying, "You want me to tell you 'bout yo' mammy, right? You love being a joker, don't you boy?" I didn't think too much about his comment and continued what I was doing.

Everyone was returning to the cottage for the day, and then another homeboy arrived. He rushed up to me and said the exact same thing. I gave him a strange look. "What the hell is going on?" I asked. I could hardly speak. I couldn't believe my ears. "That wasn't a joke? Wow!" I whispered.

"Yeah, man! Your name was on the board. You're going home next month," he repeated.

I couldn't wait for the next day to come so I could see it with my own eyes. Time moved slower than a snail at full speed ahead. I had to wait until I arrived at school to see the bulletin board. When I got to the school's door, I took off like a bullet to see it with my own eyes. I stood staring at the bulletin board, and it was just like my homeboys said. The news was real!

For a moment I got lost in a trance. I was so happy, it seemed like I had stood in a bed of ants and wanted to dance. While I rejoiced in the moment, I didn't realize the rest of the guys had headed to their classes and I was still standing in the hall.

Mr. Crockett was also a substitute teacher. If you were at The Florida School for Boys in the 1950's and didn't know him, you were at another school. Everybody knew him. I think he was the role model for the Black side of the campus. Mr. Crockett was tall and a real sharp dresser. I think he was ten years ahead of his time, and the guys on campus knew he was nobody to be on the wrong side of.

Every time we saw Mr. Crockett, he was dressed to kill, clean to the max, sharp as the end of a pin, and his shoes were spit shined. We never saw him with a wrinkled shirt or pants. He was tall and moved slow, with his shades resting on top of his head. He could have had all the women on campus if he wanted them.

Saturday morning was the time for general cleaning, from raking the yards to shining shoes, and get your clothes and shoes together. Although we were young, unlearned slaves, Mr. Crockett made sure everyone in his cottage was clean and standing tall. He had inspection every day if you were in his class or cottage. He was also a substitute cottage father. Everybody had to shine their shoes. Mr. Mobley might have been a little jealous of Mr. Crockett, and that might have been one of the reasons he beat us so severely. He stayed upset and angry with him.

"Huntly!" Mr. Crockett said. "Why are you still out here? Your name being on that board don't give you no special privileges. Come here."

"Mr. Crockett, I was just looking at the board," I said.

"Yeah, I know. Now come here."

"Yes sir," I said. I moved closer to him. I knew he was going to mall my head, and that's what he did.

I took his abuse, flinched and hurried off to class. I was going home, and I smiled because that was all that mattered. Finally! The dream that had eluded me for so long had come true. I never thought I would come out of FSB alive. The road I traveled was long, rough, and hard. I never thought the day would come that I would see the town of Marianna alive again, let alone catch a bus going back home. In October of 1958, I boarded a Greyhound bus in Marianna, Florida, to return to Orlando. After a long seventeen months of brutal struggle.

CHAPTER 19
Deno and Me

Shortly after returning home, my mother moved to the little town called Apopka (population under 10,000), right outside of Orlando. With all the things that were going on, we now had to adapt to our new home. I was fresh out of the reformatory school. Anyone who had ever experienced a government slave system wouldn't have any idea what life would be like transitioning from a caged-in world to an open, free world. Everything was different. I raise my hat to those persons who are able to withstand the pressures of that sudden jolt, of being free overnight, in a world where you have to quickly readjust. It can be scary and confusing. Many of the guys couldn't adjust to the freedom.

Life came at me like the speed of light. My name was all over town, nobody wanted to associate themselves with me because I was fresh from the reform school. Suddenly, there seemed to be no place for me to fit in. I managed, but finding that place was hard.

We were not familiar with very many people in Apopka, and we knew right away the people in that town weren't very accepting of strangers, especially those from the Orlando area. Usually, whenever youth from these two towns met, in places like school, teen dances, football games, movies, or just visiting, they would clash. Each town felt they had something to lose by having new guys in town. A lot of their girls were at risk, which was partly right. During those days it was about which town dressed the best, danced the best, and had the nicest cars. It was a contest just like schools had their spirted sports battles to decide who had the best teams.

Once we broke through the barriers and made some new friends in Apopka, we got to know people from other surrounding towns. We were known all over the place and had little to no problems in either Apopka or Orlando. Orlando was the "mother" of all the other little towns.

I was free now to explore the world—I thought so anyway. I didn't know my idea of being free was different from what the system's law intended. I was too young to know during those years that the young Black man, "colored boy" as they called us, was in danger of being stopped by the law and arrested without cause.

According to the thirteenth amendment of the United States Constitution, a person could be enslaved if they were arrested for *any* offense, and the court would find them guilty as charged. Florida changed many misdemeanor laws to felonies for the sole purpose of enslaving people of color. They were stripped of their rights and were thereby owned by the State of Florida. The court placed you wherever they wanted free labor. I didn't realize the man who kept arresting me on "general principle" was Jim Crow, the law for Black people, especially men.

My brother, Willie Jr, (Deno,) had returned home and joined us in the little town of Apopka. I called it our second home. We had gotten to know each other pretty well by then, even though we had been separated several times during our lives. My other brother, Art, was still at FSB working off an invented debt created just for him by the State of Florida.

On weekends the teens had a little more time to stay up and hang out, but it just wasn't like the city of Orlando. Orlando was the city where everything was happening, so one night Deno and I decided to head to the city where we were known. Earlier that day I found a Dutch (knife). I liked the knife and told my brother I was taking it with me to Orlando. I would come to wish a thousand times that I'd left that knife where I found.

The night we left Apopka heading to Orlando, I had no idea it would take a year or more to get there. We were hanging out with two or three people in Apopka where we lived, which was mostly a migrant working town. People usually migrated to Apopka for seasonal farm work of all kinds, working the fields with oranges, peas, corn, celery, and the like, and they were paid daily.

Around eleven p.m., the town was shutting down for the night. We would not have been able to make it back to our home before our curfew, which Mama had forewarned us about that, but to us, the night was still young. I was not quite thirteen years old yet. But remember, I had just returned home from the reform school where young boys are turned into young men overnight. Here I was stuck in the middle—too young to be an adult and too old to be a young teenager.

We began heading out to the big city of Orlando, which was about twelve miles south of where we lived. It was a spur of the moment decision, and we decided to go.

Catching a ride to Orlando seemed pretty simple since partygoers were traveling the roads all times of night. Deno knew quite a few of them from Orlando. That night there wasn't much traffic; hardly any cars were going in our direction. Highway 441 South was the popular road to Orlando from Apopka, and it still is. We walked for about forty-five minutes, give or take a little, when a policeman came from out of nowhere. He pulled over to the side of the road, his bright lights shining on our backs.

"Aw, hell!" I said. Without looking around I knew it was the police. Just as I looked back, he turned the red light on top of the police cruiser on. In the 1950's and before, the police cars had only one light on top of the car; it was a round shaped revolving red light.

"What the hell is he stopping us for?" Deno asked. "Let me do the talking, Bro."

I knew I could be sent back to the reform school, but not for walking to Orlando. That's what I thought, anyway. The policeman got out of his car and came up to within a few feet of us.

"Is there a reason for stopping us, officer?" Deno asked.

The police answered, "Well first, you don't ask the damn questions, boy, I do that. Now, I got a call saying some colored boys were spotted snooping around in one of them neighborhoods a lil' earlier, and, hea' y'all go." The policeman stood with a hand on his pistol staring at us.

Deno said, "Look officer, we just left Apopka about an hour ago. The people we were visiting can verify that. We're going to Orlando."

"I supposed you boys got a name?"

"We do," Deno said.

"What is it, boy?" Before Deno could answer that question, the police got a little loud and asked, "What the hell you boys doing out hea' this time of night?" he asked. "What you lookin' for?"

I said, "We ain't looking for nothing. We're just on our way to Orlando, like he told you."

By that time, two more policemen had driven up and gotten out of their police cruisers with their hands on their pistols, too. The cop who stopped us began to raise his voice a little louder.

One of the other two cops said to the officer in charge, "They giving you some trouble? We can take care of that for you pretty quick, you know."

"No. That's alright. Everything is under control," said the officer who had called them.

The other officer came up and said, "By God, they just **niggers**, you do know that?" It was said as if that word was a code word.

Things really got a little heated up when the first officer told him, "It won't be necessary, it's not called for."

The other cop flew off the handle as if he was upset because of the answer. "Hell, yeah it is! I just get sick of niggers running round hea' like cock roaches thinking they can do anything they want to do."

The skinny cop shook his head and said, "What's y'all's name again, boy?"

The questioning became a little more tense. Deno was quick to anger when he felt danger was inevitable. It was sure to be a fight. I was young, but after spending seventeen months at FSB, I had learned to fend for myself and if that incident would have turned into a scuffle, Deno and I would have gone down together.

"Willie Huntley," Deno responded.

Another officer looked at me and asked, "What about you, boy?" Before I could answer the question, he said, "Nigger, did you hea' me?" The other two police were standing close by with their hands resting on their pistols and looking right at me.

"Richard," I answered.

"Richard what, boy?"

I paused for a second and said, "Huntly."

"Boy, I done heard yo' name befo'," one of the cops said. I was too young for an ID card, so he went to his police car and called my name into the station. When he returned, he said, "Y'all boys find whatcha was looking for?" He looked at the officer who stopped us and said, "That little one just came back from that reform school."

Immediately, he told us both to take everything out of our pockets and put our hands on the car. I placed the little Dutch knife I found on the car. I didn't have much of anything to speak of in my pockets. He put us in cuffs and took us downtown. In my mind I knew nothing was pending on me. I just knew everything was alright. Hell, I didn't steal or drink and hadn't got into it with anybody.

The police took us down to Orlando's headquarters for questioning, but we were never questioned at all. To my shocked surprise, both of us were placed in detention and charged with walking late hours at night and carrying a deadly weapon. The final report said my brother Willie Huntley Jr. was the one carrying the deadly weapon. Deno and I were charged as "incorrigible," meaning, "can't be corrected, trained or reformed."

Judge Mattie Farmer had us returned to the Florida School for Boys' in 1958. It was the second time for each of us. We were sentenced to remain there one year or until legally released by the school or until age 21.

School Register

This additional section of The Florida School for Boys register marks Richard Huntley and Willie Huntley's return to the school in 1958. The continuation of the ledger states we were both charged as "incorrigible".

Judge Mattie Farmer was a White lady. She was responsible for placing 99% of Orlando's Black indigent boys in The Florida School for Boys; she did this without hesitation. Deno and I were no exception. Both of us were familiar with the revolving doors jeopardy. You pulled off the old you and put on the new you, the School for Boys uniform, and again became state-owned property, a slave, back to the farm mindset.

CHAPTER 20
Returned to the Boy's School
1958

*W*e arrived at the school in the evening, just like before. When we entered the revolving door at the Dozier plantation, we were taken straight to the office which was just immediately after entering the White side of the campus where the induction station was located. This part of the White side of the campus was as far as a Black boy was allowed to go. We were carried back to the Black side once our names were officially signed in at the Florida School for Boys plantation.

When the car pulled up to the office, Mr. Mitchell was waiting like always when we walked in. He knew both of us well, so the talk was short. "Richard Huntly," he said, "after all that time you stayed here, we couldn't keep you out the Grubs. Seemed like you had a problem trying to go home. You mean you left here, messed up again, and came right back? I thought you had enough of this place."

Then he turned to Deno. "Willie Huntley, it's been a long time since I've seen you. Well, I see you brought your little brother back with you this time. I am still here, and I still run this damn school without flaws. No playing, fighting, and doing what you want to do. You do what you're told. I think I still have plenty of fire power left in my right arm. What I don't have, Mobley got. Richard Huntly, didn't you just leave out of Bunche Cottage?"

"Yes, sir," I answered.

"You will go to Lee cottage this time, and the office boy will come get y'all tomorrow for your check up and shots. Willie you will go to Bethune. I think you will get along fine there. Okay!" He called the office boy to take us to the cottages. As we were leaving, he said, "I don't want to see either one of you in my office again, you know the rules. Your brother Arthur is due to leave again sometime pretty soon. You all are far enough apart that you won't be seeing each other."

When I arrived at the cottage, the guys were about to wash up and go to dinner. I jumped right in. It was hard to accept that I was really back in this hell hole again. The first evening at the new cottage, I was assigned a bunk that I felt better about. This one was located far enough back in the room, away from drafts, so I could feel warm this winter. When I was here the first time, my feet never got warm the entire winter.

Lord, it's me, Richard. I can't seem to win for losing. It seems like everything I do right, I do wrong, and everything I do wrong, I do right. Help me, please.

I was back to smiling, pretending everything was alright. The next day, I would find out what my job would be. It haunted me all night long.

Lord, wherever it is, please give me strength to carry on. This is a lot of pressure. Will I die in this place? Lord, I must try to make it out of here, so please help me control my temper and keep me from around those people that would make me loose it. Yes, it's me, Richard. Lord, I call you so much because you are the only one got time to listen. Thank you for hearing my prayer.

My first day in the mess hall, I knew just about everybody in Bunche Cottage. I saw them all in the chow line. Bunche and Lee Cottages shared the chow hall together. The guys were asking me, "What happened, Huntly?"

"Hell, I don't know."

"Where will you be working?"

"I don't know yet," I answered.

"Hey Hunt, tell them in the office you want to learn how to sew and try to get in with us. The work ain't hard at all and you could make rank. I'm for real. Tell them man. I know you can get it," one of the guys suggested.

"Hey, gotcha man. Okay, thanks." I thought that suggestion was great.

———————— ❧ ————————

We had to take shots and test for school and a job again. I don't know why. I didn't think it made sense to test us for milking cows or working in a processing plant, and certainly not to work with the field crews. For about the first three days the standard procedure was, doctor visits, test, and classroom until I was placed on a permanent job and in my regular school grade, which was still the third grade for me. I was right back with Johnny Drunk, Mr. Evans' class. It was the same routine day after day.

Deno was assigned to the kitchen detail after his shots and doctor visits, dentist, eye doctor, etc. The good thing about it was I got a chance to see Deno daily, and we ate pretty well because of him. Our brother Art could communicate with us daily through Deno.

One night in Lee cottage, before we went to bed, I clearly heard a big mouth talking about somebody being lucky enough to get out of the reform school and being stupid enough to come right back. "How dumb is that?" the loudmouth guy said.

He meant for me to hear what he was saying, and I knew he was talking about me. I had just returned to the school and I was mad as hell for being back. I approached the guy. "Hey man, you talking about me? Sounds like you might want to tell me something. If you do, got-damn-it, I am right here, talk to me!" I got right in the punk's face. I was angry and looking for someone to slap the hell out of anyway. My whole body posture also spoke for me.

"Naw! I wasn't talking about you, man," the guy retreated. He looked like he just deflated.

"Anytime you have something to say to me, I'll be here a while!" I whisper-yelled my response. I thanked God that blew over. I didn't want any trouble. I just got back and didn't want to have to go right back to the Grubs.

The next three days finally passed, and I was assigned to the sewing room. It worked out just like homie said.

I managed to get in touch with Art through Deno, and all was well with them also, but Art was still catching hell with the cow milking and catching the newborn calves.

My goal was to try and leave this school as quickly as I could by staying out the way of the staff members. I could get a grade from any staff member on campus, for anything they saw me do or heard me say.

The sewing room proved to be a good place to be to stay out of trouble. The supervisor was a very old White lady, and she knew her stuff when it came to sewing. She started me off by teaching me how to thread the sewing machine and needle, and how to fill the bobbin. It took a few days of training until I got used to how to operate everything. The next step was learning how to darn. The laundry was in the same building; I also wanted to learn how to press pants and shirts. Finally, a job I could master and understand.

When it was my time to take a break, I was about to drop from exhaustion. I took time to give thanks.

Lord, I thank you for this break. You know I didn't do anything to return back here. Thank you for this new job and not having them send me back to the fields or processing plant.

A few weeks after returning to the school, I found myself in the midst of a campus partial shutdown. One of the older guys from Louis cottage where my brother Arthur stayed did a daring thing. His named was Sol. He worked on Mr. Stevens' plow crew. Sol decided he wanted to leave the school and he did it in a rather cool and unthinkable way. Instead of running through the bushes and weeds in the woods, he decided to take one of the mules to make his getaway.

The office boy delivered the word to all the classrooms and cottages with an alert saying, "One of the guys on the plow crew took off with one of the mules." Everybody was admiring the nerve Sol had. Nobody knew how long it had been since his escape. By the time his absence was noticed, he had already been gone seven or eight hours.

The plantation's upper heads had thought no one in their right damn mind would ever try that. Well, Sol didn't just try, he did it. I marveled over his bravery. He outsmarted the school. The officials were afraid other boys would try the same thing and that would make them look incapable of maintaining control.

It was cold and winter had set in. The hunt was on and everything was quiet. I don't know where Sol's hometown was. I do know of the brutal punishment one received for attempting to escape if they didn't get away. They liked to make examples out of runaways, planting fear into the minds and hearts of all of us who might think of escaping in any way.

For the first time I saw guns being worn by the school's supervisory staff on the Black side of campus. Mr. Mitchell, Mobley, the cottage fathers, and every other staff person were on alert. Apparently, they thought if Sol was courageous enough to steal a mule, he might be bold enough to come after one of them.

There were no fences separating the plantation from the free world. The KKK were depended upon to search and capture any runaway that slipped through the school's fingers. Runaways were not expected to escape Jackson County, and they could do what they wanted to them. The campus was swarming with staff members. They rode around in the state car, on and off the grounds.

What would happen to Sol if he were captured? He was never seen or heard from again that I know of. Think of a Black boy on a mule cornered off in the woods around White Knight country, trying to find his way to freedom. This could have been a fatal situation.

The mule was returned to the farm, but Sol wasn't. Was Sol labeled a smart nigger for his bravery, or was he taught a lesson? Did he really get away, was he caught by the school's staff, or did the sheriff catch him? Did the KKK have a "pick-nick" by hanging and castrating him? Was he caught and sent to another reform school or prison? Many things could have happened to Sol. Did his family get one of those many departing letters stating, "Your son left the school and was never seen or heard from again"? Did the staff, sheriff, or KKK murder him and bury him in the woods?

I had never heard of anything like that happening before, escaping on one of the mules. Sol had only been at the school a few months, so I heard. I'd prefer to believe if Sol had enough intelligence to do that, he was smart enough to have someone waiting on him, and at the precise time he gave the state back their mule. I like to believe Sol sailed off in the wild blue yonder and he is living happily ever after somewhere outside of the State of Florida.

⌘

I had only been back at the school for two months or so and I was still angry about my situation. I was afraid to let my guard down. It seemed, whenever I relaxed, Satan was always lurking around. I don't think there was ever a time when I was relaxed. Being on alert daily was the key to surviving at the school. Completely staying out of trouble was almost impossible. I tried to do my best, but I'll be darned, the littlest thing always kicked off a bad situation.

We could use the gym on the White side of the campus when they were not using it for games, however we never played games at the same time in the same place as the White boys. We didn't have a gym on the Black side. The rule had always been the Black boys could use the facilities when the White boys were not using it.

The Black guys had a basketball game in the gym a few months after I was returned. One of the guys was sitting behind me. I don't know what he was thinking, but he kept kicking the bleachers where I was sitting. I turned around and asked him to stop. He stopped for about five minutes or so and started doing it again. Twice, I asked him to stop. The third time, I turned around to say something to him, but instead I stood and hit him in the face and continued to put his lights out. We fought. I don't know what came over me. I seemed to be angry all the time and quick to throw a blow.

I was so disappointed in myself, but it was too late. Everybody saw me hit him first, even the cottage father;

that's what did it. Needless to say, after doing so well, I still got a ride in the Blue Goose to the White House. I really didn't know what to expect to happen to me from day to day. My fourth beating at the school in a long time. It seemed like I could have melted through the floor for losing my temper.

My next school day, around five o'clock, here comes the office boy with that white slip in his hand and of course, my name was on it. I had to go to the office. Mr. Mitchell had told me not to come back to his office, and there I was. *Damn!* I thought. I finally got the strength to pull myself up off the little bench. It took all the muscles in my little body to go into the office that day. But somehow, I walked in and sat down. I was worried. What would happen to me this time? My body was broken down from this kind of brutal punishment. How long would I be able to stand this?

Lord, I don't know, but I got to hold on, hold on one more time. Please don't leave me.

There were three more guys sitting in the office just like before. Everyone was timid with nothing to say. They were trying to gather the strength it was going to take to hold that bed. Mr. Mitchell called us into the office one at a time. Two of the guys had already been in the office before I got there and the third was coming out.

"Richard Huntly!" Mr. Mitchell called out.

When I heard my name, what little hair I had, stood up on my head and arms. I felt like running, but there was nowhere to run. I felt like breaking down and crying right there, but I'm Richard Huntly and that was unheard of, at least outwardly. Inside, I was trembling. Any of the other times when I was taken to the White House, I got by without turning the bed loose. The excruciating pain was unmatched, except for being scalded with boiling hot water.

Mr. Mitchell had called my name in an angry tone; he was mad. I sat there for a few seconds. It was silent except for him shuffling papers on his desk. Then he looked over the top of his glasses directly at me. "I told you not to come back to my office, didn't I?" he reminded me.

"Yes, sir." I replied. I tried to explain but my voice began to tremble. "Mr. Mitchell, can I say something, sir?"

He looked straight in my eyes and said, "You mean you got something to say, boy?"

This was strange. I never had anything to say when I rode to the White House.

"It's a little late for that, isn't it boy? You should've thought about all of whatever you're gonna say before you hit that boy in the gym."

"Yes, sir," my voice mumbled.

"You know what you did. I told you I run this damn school and you niggers don't seem to understand that. I thought you had changed, Richard, and you had the nerve to show out in the gym where all the big, important people were looking at the game. That made it look like I can't run my got-damn school. Have a seat out there."

"But Mr. Mitchell, I didn't really start that fight," I said.

"That's not what's on this paper. Listen, I told you I didn't want to see you in my office. I hear ya. I'm gone let ya keep ya rank, but ya know what's gonna happen. Now, have a seat out there."

"Yes, sir," I said. I clenched my lips, but the heated breath of my anger blew out threw my nose.

Mr. Mobley pulled the Blue Goose around in front of the office as usual and it was time to load up. *White House, here I come.* I was psyching myself up, getting mentally prepared. It was going to be a long day, living or dead.

We loaded up for the short ride, and we arrived at the side of the White House where they always parked. Mr. Mitchell was driving; he pulled to a stop and switched off the car. I noticed one of the boys was new and it was his first time riding. I felt his pain because he was in for a rude awaking.

Mr. Mobley opened the passenger door and got out. Holding the White House's keys, he walked toward the dingy building. By now, I realized this was real, not a dream. I was so psyched up, I was ready to get it over with, dead or alive. The White House is never the same; you don't get used to a torture chamber, and only the strong-minded survived. The inside of the dark dungeon was enough to drive anybody insane.

While we stood and watched in fear, Mr. Mobley struggled to open the old solid wooden door with the four panels. It was yellowish in color with peeling paint, and there were small pine trees growing up around the building. Visitors who passed by might have thought it to be an old abandoned building that was not in use anymore. One or two windows were broken; the bathroom was smelly and hadn't been used in years. The little building used a few fifteen or thirty watt light bulbs. The door hinges needed oiling and squeaked when the door was opened.

The White boys working in their kitchen could look out the window and tell whenever someone was taken into the house. There were times Mr. Mitchell would call some of the White boys to come and hold the little Black boys down so they could be beaten. Either way, you lose when you turn the bed loose.

Once again, I heard the words, "Go in there and sit on the bed." ("In there" was the room where they beat the White boys. We had to sit on their bed while waiting our turn to be beaten on the Black boys' bed.) Mr. Mitchell gave his little speech. "I know what you did, and there is no way out, so let's deal with it. You boys know this is gonna hurt me just like it hurts you. But you are going to learn and understand boys, you do what you're told. I run this school."

I had heard that little talk before, but my mind was on another level. I'm not staying in my body today and I know I won't be slabbed like some of the other guys. My mind was charged up. *Mitchell, damn-it! Stop talking and let's do it.*

Then I heard, "You first!" but it was another guy; I didn't go first. I wished I had been first, because I was ready to finish it.

I don't remember how many licks the other guys got that day because I was worried about whether Mobley would slab me. I knew he could at any time.

Finally, it was my turn to lay on the bed. When I stood up to walk in the room with the already soaked pillow of tears, snot and slobber, I heard Mr. Mobley say, "Lay on that bed and look at the wall!" Just as I was laying on the dingy dirty mattress, he continued, "Do yourself a favor boy, don't turn lose!"

I knew I was dead. I was ready for the blood this time because all the indications were in place. The first lick, BOOM! My brain froze like always. I thought I could mentally prepare for this, but I couldn't. By the time I thought it was time for the second lick, Boom! And the third, Boom! Boom! Boom! The licks kept coming, and my mind was going crazy after about fifteen to twenty licks. By now, I was into my own inward world of prayer for help. I was in danger of being split open and my flesh pulled from my bone.

Lord help, please don't let it all end right here.

I knew Mr. Mobley could turn that strop sideways at any time and split my flesh wide open at his will. I started to sweat now and pant for breath. I was turning my head from side to side, squeezing the rail on the bed so hard I felt I could have bent it. As I lay there my whole body was trembling. I was trying to time the licks. My pain was so severe I welcomed death with open arms, but it just didn't come.

Suddenly, I heard another boy hollering out, from the power of the painful blows being delivered to my body and I realized it was someone else making that sound from hearing the electrifying blows administered to me. At first, I thought it was me, but it wasn't my sound. I moaned and groaned inside with each blow and waited for what felt like death to come and take me at any minute. The cries came from one of the other guys waiting to be beaten. Just hearing the sound of my beating scared the newcomer so bad, he panicked. By now, I think I had left my body. All I remembered was getting up in response to a loud commanding voice. When getting up off the bed, I tried to get my balance to leave the little room.

"I am alive!" I whispered to my Lord with, *"Thank you."* My next thoughts were, *am I slabbed? If so, is my behind bloody?* This beating "brought the house down" for me." I felt like my whole backside had doubled in size. I prayed to the God of our ancestors. I had survived once again and made it through another ancestral beating without being split open.

I believed the guy that was hollering so loud had to be held down before getting his beating. He was picked up and carried to the bed; that wasn't a good sign. I was in the other room while my butt was cooling off.

When we left the White House, Mr. Mitchell and Mobley drove us back to the cottages and let us out. We were in different cottages, but all of us used the same chow hall. It was usually at dinnertime when boys were returned from the White House. Our abusers wanted everyone to see firsthand those getting out of the Blue Goose, to set an example. Some of the guys needed a pillow to sit on because that pain would stay with them for at least two weeks or more.

I began to ask myself why so many beatings. My body was repaired in a week, while others took two to three weeks to heal. By that time, I wouldn't think about that beating until I had to ride again. What was it about me? I couldn't understand who I was. Sometimes that thought ran through my mind. Most guys that came to Dozier were taken to the torture chamber once, maybe twice over the period of their stay. We were all brainwashed to be good little slaves and to do whatever we were told. But four times for me? I guess I just couldn't be the little model slave boy.

After that last beating, I was determined not to experience another. It was hard staying within the rules, but it was possible. The beating was one thing, but then to be paraded into the chow hall for all to see my humiliation, that was almost as painful. I put up a front that I could take the beating, but couldn't hide the pain of moving about on sore and inflamed muscles.

⁓⁓⁓

I was still in Lee cottage. I wanted this to be the last cottage I lived in on the plantation. That last beating got my full attention. I was hopeful nothing worse would happen. I had been at the Florida School for Boys more than two years now with this trip being the second. I was destined to do one of two things, leave this place standing up and walking or laying down and riding. There were plenty of days I sat and wondered why so much pain. Most of the time, I would go to the little church on the campus. I tried to always do what I was told to do. I didn't bother anyone, and I minded my own business, but yet I stayed in more trouble than the average guy. Why?

Sure, I was fortunate enough to be working in the laundry and sewing room. The laundry was right inside the gates on the White side of campus and the White House was a few yards farther up, right around the corner. There was talk of this Black guy dying in one of the dryer tumblers. Nobody knew how he ended up in there. Someone had to put him in there and turned it on. Once the door was locked, there was no way it could be opened from the inside. It was a commercial type dryer. I never heard if they found out who did that to this guy.

Although I was in the laundry, it didn't mean I was out of trouble's reach. I just moved with a little more caution than at other times. Somehow, some way, I knew I was going to be alright, I'm not so sure what it was about me, but I always knew deep down in my gut I'd be okay, even in my darkest hour. I don't know how I knew this.

With the job in that laundry, I had time to gather my thoughts. How many more rivers of trouble did I have to cross before I reached the other side? For the first time since I was placed at FSB, I believed I was learning something that could be beneficial after I left. My mind was clear and I figured out what I needed to achieve to leave this school. I thought about leaving this place forever.

I don't know if my supervisor, the elder White lady, was scared or just easygoing. Mr. Mitchell and Mobley came through a couple times a week. I'm sure they were just checking. It didn't seem like anything could go wrong at my new job, and then all hell broke loose.

The sewing room and the laundry were two different departments under the same roof. Only four of us were in the sewing room and going to work wasn't that far. When we got to work, one of the laundry boys decided to "catch a rabbit." I didn't know what made him break for it; there was rarely someone to slip through the cracks of escaping. The next day the runner was back at the school, another example. It was pitiful to see a person beaten within an inch of his life by men who took joy in dishing out such pain on another human being. It was pitiful and unnerving to see that sight.

I began making rank for the first time at the plantation, but there were some setbacks. I think some of the school staff looked the other way for some of the things I did to help me leave. My mother was aware of the brutality that my brother Art reported to her when he was first released. The school probably thought if they killed me, my mother had grounds to make some noise and put the world on alert about what was going on.

———————— ⌘ ————————

I had been a conscientious fellow since I was a young boy. I never thought of myself as a follower, but I always liked being around my brothers. Although we had been apart most of my life, they were my world, but being around them caused me great suffering and pain since I was young and naive about things I knew nothing about until it was too late. I was being locked up and charged with a crime when I had nothing to do with it. My brothers tried to tell the police, but their words were always disregarded.

As I grew older, I realized I had a kind of "sixth sense." I could gauge a situation and think for myself before I moved forward. It was something like cause and effect: if I did this, that could happen; if I moved over there, this would happen. Having the time to find myself was quality time well spent. Simply put, I wised up. Some of the other guys would talk to me because I had been there for a long time and some of the new guys would seek my advice pertaining to survival and stories about the school itself. I shared with the newcomers who wanted to know.

God blessed me to be in a position to press my pants and shirts. Other guys in my cottage asked me to do their pants and shirts also in exchange for some of their canteen and gift boxes when they got them.

∞∞

One evening, my homeboy, Leroy, sat next to me after mealtime. Leroy's job was to drive the tub, a tractor with trailer that was used to carry food from the Black side of campus to the White side. He had to be out early in the morning while most people were still asleep. He hauled gallons and gallons of milk, pork, beef, veggies etc. At least the guys on the White side of the campus could cook their own food and the 'north campus slaves' didn't have to do that for them, too. Leroy had to make these early morning deliveries and get the hell away from the south side before daylight, when the Whites were awake for the day.

That evening Leroy's hand was bandaged. He looked like he was really hurt bad. He was favoring his hand, holding it close to his chest like it was supported by an invisible sling.

It was really cold that morning in the Panhandle of Florida; it really gets cold in the winter. Leroy told me his hands, nose, ears, and feet had no feeling in them when he reached his destination on the White side. That wasn't anything new; the majority of us felt the same thing every day. A lot of injuries happen in the winter because we worked in much colder weather than most. My hand and feet stayed cold the entire winter when I worked outside. However! Leroy said he had a funny feeling that morning that something was going to happen; his feeling just wasn't right.

Leroy said he was trying to hurry and get back to the north side so he could enjoy the warm heat before making another delivery. His hands were already stiff from the freezing weather and from driving the tractor with no gloves. He said he parked and quickly jumped off before attempting to disconnect the trailer from the tractor. In his eagerness to unhook the hitch, somehow the trailer rolled a little and his hand was caught between the trailer hitch and the tractor.

His hand was crushed. He was hollering for help from somebody, anybody, but no one came. He said he was trying to pull the trailer with one hand, but he couldn't, and somehow, with the help of GOD, whatever happened, he got his hand free.

"You know how it is when you're scared and don't know what to do?," he said. "All kinds of thoughts were going through my mind. I knew I was in danger and nobody was coming to my aid. Man, I panicked!" He held his hand out and stared at it. "Hunt, I'm telling you man, I don't know how it happened, but the strength I had was nothing but a miracle. God had to do that because I couldn't."

I think that day, Leroy was made into a believer. He was scared anyway; it was before daybreak and everything was still. However, he got his hand free. It wasn't pretty, but his hand was saved. He said he went to the dispensary (hospital) on the White side and was refused medical care. He said he could see the lights on, that was the reason he went there.

The response wasn't really a surprise. Blacks were not welcome on that side of campus. He continued, "Hunt, man! I was taking them food and they still wouldn't help me." He said they told him, "Nigger, get off this porch, dripping all that damn blood everywhere!"

He said he asked whoever answered him from the window, saying, "I got my hand hurt bringing food over here. It's hurt bad, can I see a doctor, please?" But the voice yelled back, "Go on your side and see that doctor, nigger!"

Leroy said, "Man, you don't know how mad I was. The hard cold made my hand throb even more." He said he got back on the tractor, his hand was unprotected from the cold weather and bleeding; his clothes were being soaked by now also. He said he drove back to the Black side for help. He looked at his bandaged hand again. He said a couple of his fingers had the skin peeled to the bones, it was freezing cold, and they wouldn't treat him on the White side for his injuries. He said it didn't mean anything to the people he was bringing food to. If that's not hate, what the hell is it called?

"What did that old crazy doctor at the infirmary have to say? Do you still have to drive?" I asked.

"No! Somebody else will take my place until my hand get better," he answered.

"Hey, Leroy, at least you can go to class or just hang around the job," I said.

"Whatever happens, I hope the best for you, Huntly," he said. "I heard you are making rank."

"Yeah, I'm trying to get out of here alive," I told him. "See you later."

"Alright man."

I made Pilot for the first time in my life at the school, but there were some setbacks. I managed to keep myself out of trouble for the next several months with hopes of leaving that place alive. A few months later, I had a lip battle with a guy. We had some heated words. This was bound to happen sooner or later. Well, I couldn't help myself, there was always somebody trying me, and I was trying to stay clean.

We were told by the cottage father to be sure and check the bulletin board at school for our ranking report. It was like a report card and if I were trouble free for a couple of months, the possibility of going home was great. It was time to be cool, but like I said, it was more likely the other guys would test me.

I was so happy when my name first appeared on the list to go home. I had dreams of starting a new life. It was unexplainable. I was ready. It really was a good feeling to write Mama and tell her they were letting me come home. I wanted to write and let her know they were sending me home alive. I had been waiting to write this letter a long time. Monday, my next school day couldn't come fast enough, and I finally wrote that letter.

I couldn't sleep all week before leaving. The nights were slow; it seemed like time had stopped. Then the day came for the second time. I was discharged on October 7th, 1959. One of the staff members took me to Marianna, bought a ticket, and put me on the Grey Hound Bus for the second time bound for Orlando, Florida. I couldn't believe it until I had boarded the bus. Finally, I parted ways with The Florida School for Boys for good. *I survived*.

Note

*I am a former child slave, I am limitless, I am bold and I am **FREE** to think and speak for myself.*

The pain I have experienced was like that which my ancestors felt. I experienced firsthand how they had been broken down; I know what it was like to work in the fields with the scorching sun bearing down on their heads daily and at the end of the day or workweek, not receiving one dime for their labor.

I worked my heart out in the freezing cold and scorching sun, sick and well, and my only pay was escaping with my life, and a bus ticket home. That was over two years of free labor. I know what my ancestors felt like. During my time of trial and tribulation, I followed the protocol verbatim, but still I stayed in trouble. I didn't really do anything to get all the punishments and beatings I got at FSB. I am the seed of my ancestors, and apparently I was following their path. The same slave guide taught to them over 400 years before was given to me over four hundred years later, with the same words and the same pictures therein: ***The Bible!***

Our ancestors sent me back to give this live report of a true account, the making of a slave and the pain no man can explain—no, not even JESUS himself.

PART 3
PRESENT TIME

CHAPTER 21
A Time of Reckoning

*I*n 2008, I was invited and accepted the invitation to join a group of men who were collaborating to express the conditions at the former Florida School for Boys during their confinement there. Shortly after, they went to the capital in Tallahassee to file a petition against the State of Florida. They spoke for all the men, Black, White, and other minorities, who had been treated inhumanely at the reform school which was now officially known as The Arthur G. Dozier School for Boys.

They were prepared with documented evidence of the brutal beatings, sexual assaults, subhuman working conditions, as well as information about the locations of cemeteries on the grounds where the remains of boys who were beaten to death, or died as a result of the cruel conditions were buried. These men had done their research and had recorded evidence in hand to back up their allegations. They had been traumatized and were victims of mental and sexual abuse, and severe beatings at the school during the 1950s and 60s.

Once charges were properly filed with the Florida Department of Legal Enforcement, an investigation was underway. The four former Dozier school men, one Black man and three White men, including Roger Kiser, author of the book The White House Boys, formed a group named

"The White House Boys." The mission of this organization was to include all of the men who suffered extreme abuse while confined at the reform school. The White House Boys (WHB) title came from the dirty white building where we as young boys were beaten and tortured.

I was invited to join the WHB organization by my late friend James Edward Griffin of Apopka, Florida. I agreed with the allegations and had also been a victim of the abuse, so I was very excited and jumped at the opportunity. I asked my brother Arthur to also join the group.

At this time, Dick Colon was the president of the WHB. This was an interracial organization; however, the general period of most of our experiences at FSB aka the Dozier School spanned the era of the early 1950's through the late 1960's, a period when Jim Crow laws were in effect in Florida and other parts of the country. Our most common threads were the severe punishments and abuses that were delivered with forceful intention, leaving all of us with overwhelming physical and emotional scars.

During the first two or three years, WHB met annually for a reunion. I never realized it would ever be possible to file a case against the State of Florida for violating our civil and human rights, but we all signed with attorneys Masterson, Holland and Knights, LLP.

During the reunions, I met most of the guys in the organization, and we hit it off as a group. Then, Mr. Dick Colon stepped down as president due to personal reasons. Temporary leadership was passed on within the group, and finally to the current president, Mr. Jerry Cooper. While under Mr. Colon's leadership, all members were kept informed of all matters of legal interest, as well as issues and events that occurred and were discussed in private meetings concerning the Dozier group. Under the new president, we only received updates from the lawyers once a year or for even longer periods. I was curious for more updates and information as situations unfolded.

By the third year, I began hearing about private meetings held within the year that we, the Black members, were not informed of. We only received updated information from a few "third party" men about the discussions or the outcomes of those meetings. It was during the third annual reunion of the WHB that I learned that when the media asked about the Black men who were previous occupants at the school, one White member informed them that the Black men were either in hell or in jail. Within a few months a news reporter confirmed this statement.

That information was shocking, humiliating, and a demeaning untruth, especially when considering the large number of Black men who were active members in the group at the time. It was evident, but not surprising, that Jim Crow attitudes were still alive, active, very strong, and could not be put aside even for a group of men who had suffered similar abuses and held the same common scars.

Shortly thereafter, the organization Black Boys at Dozier Reform School was organized. Several of the Black men broke from The White House Boys organization; however, a few elected to continue with their membership.

In spite of this separation, a few of the White men from the White House Boys continued their relationship with me, keeping me informed of related issues, events, and meetings in honor of our genuine friendship and in honor of The Black Boys at Dozier organization.

There are several White men, previous Dozier occupants and members of The White House Boys, whom I consider my respected friends: Roger Keiser, who always raised my name high, and who donated his time to write the forward for this memoir. Captain Bryant Middleton, who has always made sure my name and the Black boys of Dozier have been present in meetings we were not invited to. Robert Straley and Bob Baxter. These are just a few of the honorable men of The White House Boys.

I also want to express my unending gratitude to the late Mike Sapp, my special friend, whom I was proud to call my brother, and who was one of many men who supplied me with a sound friendship and inside information. When other White House Boys would not speak on the Black men's behalf, he would. He would call me in the late evening to just talk about our legal issues and events scheduled on the Dozier campus. He even stood next to me on the courthouse steps in the town of Marianna when I spoke out against a human rights situation, saying, "I am with you brother." He used to say, "I am White, but I am right, and I'm willing to battle if need be. I am armed to the max. I got your back!"

I was surprised our friendship had grown that much. I had the upmost respect for Mike and his family, and wherever or whenever the group met, he and I always got together and shared what had happened since we last saw each other.

During my early years, all of us as minors, White and Black, were separated by an unjust system, and we were unable to form lasting friendships. This injustice could never prevail. The lessons we've learned together are invaluable, and the respect we have for each other cannot be measured. As a matter of fact, I have met even more friends through The White House Boys, too many to mention. Whenever we see each other we still get along.

--------------- ༄ ---------------

There is no doubt the Black boys at Dozier suffered a more severe punishment than the White boys. We were all segregated and treatment at the school was extremely unequal. While the White boys sat and worked in a heated building, the Black boys provided the functional operation for the school by supplying food from the fields, dairy milk, and meat from the processing plant.

The Black boys were in charge of delivering food and supplies to the White boys' side of the campus at four o'clock in the morning, in the freezing cold, while they were still asleep in their beds and had no idea of the weather conditions. We worked the fields while the White boys went to school and continued their education. It was ironic that they were assigned as teacher assistants in the heated or cooler air-conditioned classroom comfort while the Black boys were forced to endure slave-like conditions even during extreme weather circumstances.

The Black Boys at Dozier organization was established in 2012. During my stay at Dozier, I was aware that White boys were housed on the south campus, but I never saw any of them to speak of. The most information I had about the south campus was relayed to me decades later by my White associates when I was a member of The White House Boys organization. With the noted exceptions of their missing boys and of the sexual and physical abuse they suffered, I believe, for them, their Dozier experience was more like that of a private boarding school.

I would never compare a group of people who lived a life of luxury compared to that of a slave and call it the result of a fair and impartial judicial system. No White man who had not walked in a Black slave boy's shoes as a child at Dozier could ever be qualified to speak for them. We are not in need of a spokesman who was a former White detainee from the same segregated school in that era, who also benefited from the Black boys' sweat and labor.

The current president of The White House Boys is definitely not qualified to make any decisions for the Black men, especially when he stood before Congress and the world and stated that all he wanted from the State of Florida was an apology and that would make his soul happy! An apology cannot begin to suffice as atonement for the Black boys who were so inhumanely used for slave labor and so violently abused for the least little thing, or for nothing at all, while the State of Florida was making millions off our free labor.

If they would just admit they were wrong for treating us the way they did, **and** compensate us – the still living and the families of the dead – for our slave labor, that would be a very healing balm. They can never put a fair value on the years we spent as slaves at FSB/Dozier, but we certainly deserve much more than nothing!

No, the State of Florida decided that what the White Boys wanted – an apology – was enough! And not one damn red cent to compensate today's living survivors, Black *or* White men (as far as I know).

It should also be noted that the members of the WHB did not vote for Florida's apology. That call came from J. Cooper, the president, without the endorsement of his constituents. It is also worth noting that if any compensation for the survivors is allocated, nothing would be allocated for the descendants of deceased men. The surviving men now range between the ages of 60 to 80 and have one foot in their grave and the other on a banana peel. The lawsuit was filed in 2008. It is evident the State of Florida was simply and stalling for time to allow the plaintiffs to die.

When pictures were shown of the White House, White grave markers, and contented groups of White boys participating in various activities, the public was given a misleading impression. These conditions were published and broadcasted throughout the media, as well as aired on the internet through documentary digital videos. The pictures that were presented support the false concept that only White boys were sent to the school. Where are the pictures of the north side of the school, the segregated section where the Black boys lived? Where are the pictures of the disparity between the unequal educational systems, assignment of working conditions, medical infirmaries, and housing units?

There are a variety of reasons why White boys were sent to Dozier. I've heard their stories, but I can only speak for the Black boys. As stated earlier, most of the Black boys came from indigent families where parents were, in many cases illiterate; at the very least, they didn't have a clear understanding of how the State of Florida could and would confiscate their sons and send them unto slavery that was overall just as oppressive and deadly as any period of slavery ever was.

The 13th Amendment to the Constitution of the United States is clear:

Section One

Neither slavery nor involuntary servitude, except as a punishment for crime whereof **the party shall have been duly convicted**, shall exist within the United States, or any place subject to their jurisdiction.

Most of the Black boys on the Dozier plantation had been enslaved without "Due Process" of the law. Simply put, they/we were enslaved without a formal court proceeding wherein they would have to have been convicted of a crime. A judge simply signed them into the system without parental or legal representation for charges that were not against the laws of the United States of America. For most Black boys, their rights were violated for minor offenses if any, such as, walking through a White neighborhood, smoking cigarettes, running away from home, or simply cursing and other lessor offenses. Even if the violation of more serious offenses occurred, such as, stealing, fighting, assault, or even murder, each boy was still supposedly guaranteed Due Process of the law.

We were picked up simply for being Black and poor. We were considered and treated as less than human and fit for nothing else but manual labor. The State of Florida had found a source of free labor.

In my case and as well as Art's, no trial or hearing was ever held for the charges against us. I don't know the situation or conditions leading up to Deno's detainment. Neither Arthur, myself, our mother, nor any legal representative was present when a judge signed our rights away. The State of Florida enforced their illegal system to ensure free labor through a functional system of slavery. Mrs. Alexander was one of many truant officers. They were an integral part of this unlawful system.

CHAPTER 22
May Peace Be Upon Them

*A*ny controlled system of human services has its share of casualties. There were some deaths documented at the Dozier Reform School during its 111 year history. There was and continues to remain a significant number (about 138) boys presumed dead, yet the number of human remains that have been located in unmarked graves discovered on the grounds at this time numbers only fifty-five.

What was strange for the school was not keeping documentation of the deaths, cause of death records, or documentation of the boys who presumably ran away. All of this only led to a cover up of abuse, murder, rape, and the failure of the State of Florida failed to protect the innocent juveniles on their plantation.

All supervisors associated with the school in the 1950s and 60s are assumed to be dead. As these investigations unfold, reports from others who were teens and preteens stated that many of the young boys lost their lives as a result of the severe beatings, others for simple little things such as insubordination, even in times when they were in real danger. Some lost their lives trying to protect others by reporting the abuse to the wrong authorities. Some were runaways, trying to return to their homes to escape the cruel punishments, while others had their lives taken by other boys during waged forced fights, or were hung to trees and beaten nearly to death because they refused to fight.

In 2011, The Arthur G. Dozier School for Boys was closed. In 2012, the State of Florida finally awarded a permit for anthropologist Dr. Erin Kimmerle and her team to begin the archeological work and excavation on the reform school grounds.

On January 19, 2016, the University of South Florida in Tampa released its final report on the fifty-five unmarked graves discovered. These graves were located on the north side of the facility where the Black boys were housed. Understanding the Jim Crow laws of the era, even in death, a White person would not be buried and integrated with Blacks in a known Black cemetery.

The complete reports from The University of South Florida (USF) may be located at the following website:

http://news.usf.edu/article/articlefiles/6693Cabinet% 20Update%20Dozier%20Jan%202015.pdf

In April 2019, and with the use of ground penetrating radar detectors, an additional set of twenty-seven remains were located. At first it was believed these were human remains; however, a final report was issued stating the remains were those of animals.

It is still my belief there are other burial sites on the grounds because the discovery of only fifty-five remains is a far cry away from the number of suspected missing boys. Follow the link below to read the report:

*https://video.search.yahoo.com/yhs/search;_ylt=Awr
EZ7DLC75dlDEAoQoPxQt.;_ylu=X3oDMTByMjB0aG5z
BGNvbG8DYmYxBHBvcwMxBHZ0aWQDBHNlYwNzYw?
p=27+more+suspected+bodies+und+on+dozier+school
+grounds&fr=yhs-iba&hspart=iba&hsimp=yhs-1*

CHAPTER 23
In Memory of My Good Friend Leo Collier

The oldest member of the Black Boys at Dozier Reform School organization was Mr. Leo Collier. All five members of the Black Boys at Dozier swore to each other that the five of us were a brotherhood.

Mr. Collier was present on many trips to Dozier as well as to the capital. At 82 years old, he was dependable and never missed a meeting, no matter where it was held. He walked with the aid of a cane. The capital building in Tallahassee had long hallways, but that didn't stop Leo. He would walk as far as he could, then stop, rest, and start walking again. We tried to find wheelchairs, but there just weren't any, so we took turns staying with him while he rested.

I am proud to say his daughter, Mrs. Omega White, never left him. She would drive all night to make sure Leo got to where he needed to be on time. As time·went on, Handy Man had to resign from the group, but he was still considered our brother and he was supportive of our book, Dark Days at Dozier. Leo wanted his story to be told; he wanted people to know. I promised him that whenever I had a chance to speak about The Florida School for Boys, I would continue to tell his story.

I am honored to say Leo made me feel like a real friend. I'm reminded of a meeting we had in Marianna, Florida. He arrived a little late, but when they got to the church, Omega came inside and told me Leo wanted me to come to the car. He wanted me to help him into the church. I don't know why he took such a liking to me, but he did.

Whenever he and I were together, it was "fit-na" be some shit talking! See, Leo lived in Orlando for a while years ago. He and I used to visit some of the same places. Soon after, he moved to Lakeland, Florida. First, he lived with his daughter and later in a nearby nursing home. He promised when he was able to drive again, he would come back to Orlando to see me and we were going back to whatever places that were still standing that he remembered. I promised to go visit him, and I did.

Leo would call my name out loud no matter where he was, once he knew I was nearby. He was hard of hearing, so he spoke loudly. He didn't care where he was. I'd have to go see what was going on because he wouldn't stop calling, saying things like, "***RICHARD!*** GOT-DAMN! WHERE RICHARD AT? SHIT! TELL THAT DAMN RICHARD COME GET ME! THAT'S MY BLACK ASS DAMN BUDDY!"

I asked him one day, "Leo, why the hell you call me all the time and what the hell you be wantin'?" I knew he wouldn't wear his teeth or his hearing aids, so in addition to speaking very loudly, he slurred his speech.

He answered, "'CAUSE I KNOW YO' BLACK ASS AIN'T SCARED TO TALK AND TELL 'EM WHAT YOU FEEL LIKE!"

Leo was still a part of Black Boys at Dozier the day we made history in the Governor's chambers. This was the day the Governor's office agreed to sign documentation giving Erin Kimmberle, Anthropologist from the University of South Florida, permission to exhume the bodies from the Dozier grounds. They recognized all the former residents of Dozier as well as The Black Boys at Dozier Reform School group.

Mr. Leo Collier, the oldest known survivor of Dozier, was recognized first and foremost by Mrs. Pam Bundy, Florida's State Attorney. She acknowledged him by his full name and expressed her pleasure at meeting him. She apologized for his suffering. She expressed her understanding that so many years ago there was no real reason for his treatment other than his being a young Black boy. Then she turned and with a gentle nod, she bowed her head to all of us.

I smiled. I could identify with my good friend, and I could feel his pain. He was abducted without cause in 1944 and released in 1947. I filled that spot exactly ten years later in 1957, the year The Florida Industrial School for Boys' name was changed to The Florida School for Boys. I was an eleven-year-old boy.

As a child, Mr. Collier was picked up in Clearwater for not going to school. His mother was told they were taking him to another school, and she didn't have a say in the matter. He told me, "They took me to the Florida Industrial School. Things were really bad in 1944 to 1947."

My good friend asked me to tell his story if he were no longer around. I went to see him as promised, once at his daughter's home, once at the nursing home, and finally at his funeral location.

When I saw him at the nursing home, he was still the Leo I remembered. His daughter said he talked about me all the time, so she wanted me to surprise him and wake him up. He was asleep in his wheelchair. Well, I did just that, and when Leo opened his eyes, everybody in the nursing home knew I was in the house.

In his loudest voice Leo sang out, "**RICHARD!** GOT-DAMN! YOU DID BRING YOUR BLACK ASS BACK TO SEE ME, DIDN'T YA? YEAH, YOU CAME BACK, BOY! I KNOWED YOU WAS GON' DO WHAT YOU SAY! I KNOWED IT! SHIT! YOU GON' TELL MY STORY I TOLD YOU 'BOUT WHAT HAPPENED TO ME TOO?"

I told him, "Yeah, if you're not here and I am, I will." During that visit I bet he introduced me to damn near everybody in there, including the nurses. Everybody knew him.

In Mulberry, Florida, my brother and I couldn't find the funeral in progress, so we got there a little late. We were only at the repast. How regrettable.

Leo wanted the world to know about him, how he was treated at the Florida Industrial School for boys. I believe that worried him for almost seventy years, waiting to tell somebody about what happened to him while he was there. My promise to him was, I'd tell his story to the world whenever time permitted. He asked me to tell it because he believed it had to be told.

Before he died, Mr. Collier said he never got the chance to really talk about a lot of things because nobody would believe him or understand what he was talking about unless they had been there.

This is the story Leo wanted the world to know.

"First off, that place was nothing like a school they say it was. They worked us from early in the morning till late in the evening, almost dark. I was working on the log crew. We cleaned land, planted vegetables, and built more cottages. In the winter, some of the boys who wore out their shoes had to work partly barefoot in the freezing cold weather."

Leo continued his story, saying, in 1947, before they finally released him, he was working in the field, just a normal workday with the logging crew. They had no thought that anything was wrong.

He described the overseer as a crippled, middle aged White man who walked with a cane. One leg seemed to be a little shorter than the other. On this particular day, the overseer called him. Leo said he could still hear that call, "Com-mere, boy!"

All of the other boys stopped working and looked around as the overseer was pointing that walking stick at him. "I said com-mere, boy. You!" Leo said the overseer yelled out.

Leo walked toward the overseer, and just as he got within reach of him, the overseer put the straight part of the cane in his right hand, he took a few steps toward Leo, then reached out and hooked his stick around Leo's neck. He snatched Leo so hard he fell on the ground in front of the man.

As he tried to get up, the overseer drew that cane back as far as he could and hit Leo on the muscle between his neck and shoulder. Leo lifted his hand and placed it on the base of his neck to show me where he was hit. He said when the overseer hit him, it seemed to temporarily paralyze him from the neck down.

Leo said he didn't really know what was happening to his body. All he could do was lay on the ground. He heard everything around him, but he was unable to move or respond to any commands.

Within a few minutes, he began to feel his body again, but he was still numb and barely able to function. The overseer walked up and stood over him and spoke again. "Now git up off that ground nigger, and git yo' Black ass back to work."

Leo told me he was quiet, unsteady, and in a daze the rest of the day. It took him that long to fully recover from that blow. He said he did some serious praying to God, to do one of two things for him. "Please send me home or take my life." That happened not long before his release in 1947.

As the years passed, I can't say if the effects of that attack worsened and were the basis of his physical disability and mobility issues.

Although Leo was not a part of the group anymore, his daughter, Omega and I kept in touch on a regular basis. In 2013, with three other FSB/Dozier survivors, I co-authored a book titled Dark Days of Horror at Dozier: Rapes, Murders, Beatings and Slavery. When it was published, I contacted Omega about getting him a copy. She ordered two copies right away and she and Leo insisted on paying for them; they wouldn't take free copies.

I sent the books and he was so happy because, even though his story wasn't in the book, his group was, and he had made history right along with us.

No one could touch that book. It was with him wherever he went. He had the book with him when he quietly slipped away from this life on May 9th, 2015. It was a pleasure to have had Mr. Collier as a friend, and an honor to have had him as a member, the oldest member of the Black Boy's at Dozier Reform School group. May peace be upon you, my old friend. I am still telling your story as promised.

R.I.P.

Mr. Leo Collier, 85 years old.
Slipped away from this life May 9th, 2015.

CHAPTER 24
A Return to Dozier

*M*arch 2018, I received a phone call, which I believed was from the Florida State Department. The caller offered me an invitation to an April 6, 2018 event on the grounds of the former Dozier School. This event would highlight the final opening of The White House, also known as The Ice Cream Factory, which had been a historical and very haunting part of my past. I must say I was caught by complete surprise, but welcomed and appreciated the call. Usually, I didn't get calls from the State Department and I was excited. Later, it came to my attention that my invitation had come by way of The White House Boys' president, who had planned the trip as well as the itinerary for the event.

About a week later I received another call from the president of The White House Boys. He repeated the information given earlier. Then he added, "Richard, I wanted to call and let you know we are going to Marianna for the men who have not seen inside of The White House or visited the campus since they left the school."

For me that was not a problem, actually I thought it was a great idea. Then he repeated himself saying, "We are scheduled to visit April 6, 2018, but I must warn you, Richard, there will be police on the property to keep the peace. Anybody who gets rowdy will be thrown off the property in a heartbeat. It's for everybody's protection—they will remove you."

"That's fine with me, but why are you telling me this?" I replied.

"Well Richard," he said, "I know you've had problems with some things. I've heard about it, and I just want to let you know it doesn't matter to me. But the State is giving us this opportunity before the place is closed for good. This trip is about closure for some of us."

"Listen," I responded, "you know me as well as I know you and everyone else. I told you I'm not going to start anything. As long as no one says anything negative to me, we don't have a problem."

"I just want you to know, that goes for anybody," he said.

"Ok, I'll see you on April 6th," I promised.

After that conversation I didn't really know what to expect. I was left baffled to some degree, but I was still excited about the event. There was a pretty large list of Dozier men participating, Black and White.

Again, about a week later, give or take a day or two, I received a call from another one of the leaders, who talked about the request of the men in the group to view the campus before the place was sold. I thought this was a great idea because the old Dozier plantation was actually transferred to Jackson County in Marianna. I was getting a little concerned about those calls. This call was a little different, it was a little more informative.

Prior to revisiting the school, as mentioned earlier, I had spoken with several prior residents of Dozier, who dared to even talk about their experiences and what took place there. Some of them vowed they would never return to the deadly campus. The life-threatening abuse they suffered had seriously affected each of those men and they would not return to visit, or ever enter The White House again. That was unfortunate, but I knew I had to go back; I had to revisit The White House, although I thought it would never be possible for me to willingly enter that death chamber again on my own, not in this lifetime.

I drove to the hotel in Marianna on Friday, April 5, 2018, arriving around 4:00 pm. The president of the WHB met me at the door with an additional reminder of my earlier briefing of security. I was determined to think positive, and I continued on my way.

Minutes later, I met two Black men who were standing close by. It turned out they were cousins and actual farm hands at The Florida School for Boys, who were released a few months before I was sent there in 1957. We spent a little time together getting to know each other and speaking about our various experiences while at the school. The warning telephone calls about this trip were still baffling to me. At the time, I couldn't figure out how it related to me or what was in store for me.

Early the next morning, April 6th, everyone lined up and signed a waiver stating visitors would not hold the State of Florida responsible for any accident or harm they might incur while touring the state property. I didn't know why this was necessary. We were never in any danger, but the safety briefing took place anyway. Everyone was asked to board the waiting buses instead of driving their cars to the site, but some of the men disregarded the request and drove their cars anyway. We were asked to stay away from unsafe buildings and were also informed that all weapons were prohibited on the property.

Everybody loaded onto the buses and we were driven to the church on the White side of campus for the orientation. I made it clear I was of Muslim belief and didn't care to attend services or church for prayer. I refused to enter the church service. The president and I had some words, and finally, I was asked to not start anything. I was asked to please just step inside. I could stand at the front door and not in the church because no one could stay outside for security reasons. I agreed.

They were finally finished with the introduction and orientation. We were ready to move on to the next event, the White House. Every man who wanted to visit the inside of the White House for personal closure was welcomed. Some of us had suffered a near-death experience at the hands of the oppressor, including me. We looked, touched the walls, and those who needed to get their fears and tears out of the way so they could move on with their lives.

This is the church on the White side of the campus. This church has been there for years. Credited to the Florida Memory. April 6th, 2018

Here I'm standing in what was also known as the Ice Cream Factory. As many years as it has been, the look and smell of it made me cringe.

The picture above is inside the deadly White House in real time, sixty-two years later. We were flogged in the very spot I am standing in; my shaking never stopped until it was over and I knew I was alive. Blood is still on the walls. I could still hear, "Don't turn that bed loose!" "Ok Huntly, you first!" I could also remember Mr. Mobley standing in the next room waiting on me. How many deaths occurred here remains unknown. Credited to: Richard Huntly, 4/6/18.

I believed this visit was worth the trip to see inside of The White House along with the other men. It was worth it to return to this place for my own closure. I understood the stories told by the older men who were there and spoke of it in such fearful ways. Their voices trembled as they struggled to get their words out. I could barely hear what they had to say. Those old men spoke about the fear of this place.

I heard old Black men who served there a few years before me, speak about the White House; they used their hands as though they were handkerchiefs to wipe away the tears rolling down their faces. One man, whose lips kept trembling, spoke of the dangers of the White House. He said to me, "Some who were taken there met their fate and afterward were laid to rest. So many others were beaten almost to death and barely escaped with their lives."

Fearful and trembling lips tell no lies. I was there, too. I am one of those slaves who passed through the same hallways, laid on the same filthy bed with tears in my eyes, snotty nose, and was beaten like the-slave I was. That was a pain no man could describe. I know what it means to say, "I'd rather be dead," because I know what the hurt from a fiery whip felt like when that pain shot up in your bones.

I believe I'm qualified to know the doom my ancestors felt when they were forced to crawl on their knees and beg, "Master, please!" I felt the pain they felt. See, I remember how the original White House looked in the 1950s. It's a little spruced up outside, but the same inside as it looked to those who were there before me. That trip was history in real time, and it was my least favorite day.

These are the cottages on the White side of Dozier campus still in their pristine condition today in April 2018.

It was the second part of the day that gave me the answers to all the phone calls I had received. Suddenly, what the president whispered to me before leaving the church began to make sense. "This is the best I could do," he said, as he walked past me.

The bus we were riding in explored the entire White side of the campus. The White men marveled over building after building. They called out where they stayed or what building this or that was and what took place at each location. The yards were still being manicured, new roofs were on all the buildings, and the mess hall was preserved; everything was still in pristine condition. The gym was in ready to go condition. I got in a fight in that same gym. Sixty years later, it was still in pristine condition.

Some of the White guys made it sound as if they actually missed the place. One of them who resided in one of these cottages more than sixty years ago pointed out a possible place they called the 'rape dungeon'. I was really shocked at some of their attitudes. We spent a couple hours touring the White side of the campus. Now, I'm thinking, it's time to tour the Black side of the Dozier campus, the segregated farm side; there were only four or five buildings left to tour.

The bus driver drove through the little narrow road and the view of the dilapidated buildings were visible, but there was no mention of them.

There was an empty space where Bunche Cottage once stood. The mess hall was still there, but hardly recognizable because of the kudzu vines. Lee Cottage, if my mind serves me correctly, was the next building in line. All of the cottages were very similar in appearance; it was hard to tell one location from another. Mr. Mitchell's office was located across the street from the cottages; that's where we reported in the evening and the decision was made whether we would go to the White House; the answer was yes, more often than not. There were remnants of it also. Everything else was in a dilapidated condition. "No Trespassing" signs had been placed near each building. I suspect they were necessary for safety reasons.

This Church is on the Black side. I attended this same church often. In 1959, through a dream, I died and my funeral was held here. I attended the funeral and saw my body as everyone else did. The choir song their hearts out at my home-going.

The narrow road cut right by one of the Black cottages, but the bus driver just continued driving past it. I was bothered and asked the bus driver why he didn't stop so the

Black guys on the bus could see where we were once housed. All of the White men on that bus were like us—just as we had never seen the White side of the campus, they had never seen the Black side.

The remaining view of those standing structures would have also been closure for a grieving family that had driven more than four hundred miles to get to Dozier. Their brother and uncle, Billy Jackson, was killed at the school 1952 when he was just 13 years old. His remains were among the fifty five sets that were exhumed, one of the few that were identified. In 2016, his remains were returned to his family in St. Petersburg, Florida, to receive a proper burial.

Scarcely a year and a half later, Billy Jackson's family was invited on this trip. Ironically, the same president of The White House Boys who denied Billy Jackson's family closure by visiting the site where he died, was the same person who attended and spoke at his funeral and placed a White House Boy's flag on his grave.

The Boot Hill Cemetery was directly behind Bunche and Lee Cottages, and it was the driver's next destination. When we arrived, I asked the bus driver what his next stop was. He told me the president told him when we left the cemetery to head back to the hotel. I said we needed to stop ahead and explore the Black side. The bus driver said he had to get permission. He stood in the bus's entrance and told me he would be right back. Then he left the bus supposedly to find the president of The White House Boys, Jerry Cooper, to find out my answer. A few minutes later he returned and said the president had already left and he had to do as he was originally told.

At that point, I was one angry Black man. Once again, the president of the White House Boys purely disrespected the Black men on the bus and the Jackson family. He didn't have the courage to ride the bus with the rest of us. Suddenly, the phone calls, the warnings, the invitation, the racist tour, and the police escort on the property made obvious sense. It was all for me, knowing full well that if I had known the set up they were pulling on us, it was going to be a problem. Most likely, the only reason a few of us Blacks were invited was because the White men could not get a permit from the state to visit the grounds if the former Black Dozier men weren't invited and included in the planning.

By the time the bus returned to the hotel the president had left. All the Black men and some of the White men knew this was a definite setup. Some of the White brothers told me they never saw anything of the Black side and that would have been a good opportunity to see the place where we caught so much hell.

When I returned to my home, I called the president to have a word with him. He hung the phone up on me when I questioned his motives about the tour's plan. I deserved an explanation and I was angry. I want to know why, and I am still waiting on the reason for his actions that day. That incident is still fresh in my mind. I really want to know what the hell happened.

゜⧟゜

Earlier in 2017, I was on a business trip in the Florida panhandle, and my trip took me through Marinna, right by the Dozier school. It was possible I wouldn't be passing through that area again soon, so I decided to stop by and check the old Dozier plantation once more. That visit would only add to the couple of trips we made to the old school already and I was familiar with the area. I wanted to take pictures of the old buildings for the historical future.

It was obvious then that the kudzu vines were in control and running rampant, smothering the crumbling buildings on the Black side of campus. The old Dozier school was still without a fence to keep the public off the property. When I drove onto the campus, I passed by an alternative school built near the Black church and close to the dilapidated cottages.

Minutes after I exited my SUV with camera in hand, a sheriff's deputy was heading toward me. He approached and politely proceeded to tell me that no one was allowed to enter the property any more at will. I said I understood and told him it wouldn't happen again. I asked if it was alright to continue to take a few pictures. I told him I was once housed at the school as a pre-teen slave, and pictures of the old buildings were for historical purposes. He said okay this time, but visitors had to be cleared by the main office located at the new alternative school, and they would have an official escort while looking around and taking pictures. Those conditions indicated to me that the property was about to be transferred or sold.

The officer was pretty cool and professional. As a matter of fact, we agreed to contact each other if we were ever in each other's area in the future. He escorted me around the area so I could take my pictures.

Many bad memories lingered about the hard times during this period of my life when oftentimes I lived from day to day not knowing what to really expect. Work and school were a given. In the adjacent picture (I believe) is Louis Cottage. I was thirteen years old, and I think this is the cottage a friend of mine, Nate, told me about. He said he would be placed there and had to agree to night burials or night fights for the White folk under the old oak tree or die. I was told a lot of money was made under that oak tree from forced fights of Black boys. As life would have it, I managed to make it out just in time.

Today this building is called A Ghost House. Photo Credited to Michael E. Miller Miami New Times 2/15/15.

Nate Dowling's Story

My brother Art and I attended one of the White House Boys' reunions in Tallahassee in about 2009, maybe 2010. That year, I was caught by surprise. My friend Nate, a Black man who I had previously met, was named the vice president of the White House Boy's organization. This was only in name, just a pat on the head. This position was not in writing, and surely he was not recognized as the vice president. I told him that I've always believed he was being used as a publicity stunt to draw more Black men into this organization.

I knew when some of the guys came together and started drinking, they began talking and telling about their experiences at the school. Some of them were genuine and some were full of shit. Most of them usually talked in their little segregated huddles. This practice still works today as it did yesterday among ethnic groups.

When the Black guys started talking about some of the experiences they encountered at the plantation school, Nate would be talking, drinking, having a good time, and suddenly, he would be in tears. It was obvious, something was deeply bothering him. I wasn't around him constantly; he lived in South Florida. However, he would frequently call me to talk. I didn't know what was really worrying him.

Nate came to me at the reunion and asked if he could talk to me. I said, "Yeah man, what's going on?" He had never told me he heard of me when he was in Marianna back in1959, which was the year I left. He said we were there at the same time and he remembered hearing about me. I questioned his memory after sixty plus years. As he talked, his voice trembled, and water filled his eyes. He spoke of what happen to him at the school. He took a drink of liquor and said, "Huntly, you wonder why I always like to talk to you?"

Again, I said, "Yeah, I do, what's going on Nate?"

He said, "Man, something happened to me back then. I can't get over it and I never told nobody. This thing is killing me, it's so heavy. I can't hold it no more, Huntly."

As he begins to talk, my brother Art and one more of the brothers approached. Three of us were present when he told me what broke him down after so many years. I was shocked that he remembered me from that far back. He never knew me personally and I didn't remember him.

Nate began to tell me of the untold truth. He said, "Huntly, you might have known the boy. He was in Lee cottage; that's how I knew you so well. He used to talk about you all the time and how nobody bothered you and your brothers. Huntly, man, they killed him! They killed him right in front of my eyes and I couldn't help him! All I could do was cry! I still see his eyes looking at me for help and I couldn't. Huntly, man, they would have killed me, too, if I moved to try and help him. They held the gun on me!"

I asked Nate one question, "Why was he killed?"

"The boy refused to follow through on the "underground assignment." I was looking in his face when he died, man! When I got home, I started drinking and I can't stop. I didn't know anything else to do, man. I wanted to die. I wasn't man enough to tell his people what happened to him and I was right there looking at the whole thing. We were friends and it's been killing me for years. I knew his family. I never told anybody, but y'all. His name was James. Do you remember that name, Huntly? I told you, that's how I knew you. He transferred from your cottage and then disappeared. That was him."

I said, "Nate, I think I do, but it's been so many years, man. I can't say for sure."

"Well," he said. "You were next in line, man. I'm glad you didn't get transferred to Louis cottage before you left to go home."

After hearing this from him, I asked how all those things were going on around me without my knowledge. I had two brothers there at the same time as me, why didn't I know about the 'underground assignment'?

He said, "It all started in Louis Cottage, Huntly. That was your next stop. You know the "underground assignment" meant you were going to have to bury somebody if it came up, or fight somebody in a paid midnight fight under that big oak tree for the big time White folk from downtown and the surrounding towns, or die." He went on to imitate them saying, "You know; my nigger boy is badder than your nigger boy!"

"Was it Black against White fighting, or just Black on Black?"

He didn't say if it was or not, but big time White folks were there. He did tell me my older brother Willie knew about it, but Willie never told me to expect anything out of the ordinary. He worked in the kitchen and I never had the chance to talk with him quietly; I only saw him when I was in the chow line, and I never got a message from him. Nate's story was very believable.

After a few minutes of sobbing, Nate began to catch hold of himself. The other guys dropped their heads in sorrow. "Uh, uh, uh," one of them said as they walked off.

I stayed with Nate and in a few minutes, he looked at me and said, "Of all these years, Huntly, I've never been able to tell nobody that until today. Telling y'all made me feel like a brand-new man. I think I could live in peace now. Thank you."

A year or so after that conversation, I found out why Nate knew something I didn't. He was telling me the truth. Out of my two brothers, I was next on the list. My name would ring in the death game, and I found out why. My brother Willie Jr. and I were listed as 'incorrigible' colored boys. In the Juvenile and penal system, our life wouldn't be worth investigating if one of us died, because we were listed as troublemakers and unfit to be a slave.

In the 1950's I am sure, it wasn't a big thing to hear somebody from one cottage or another had taken off from campus. Almost every day, the rumor was that some guys came back, and some didn't. Some of the older guys knew what was going on for sure. I think the threat of death and being sent to prison was what kept a lot of their mouths shut; fear was the controlling factor. A few of the guys who survived the school in the fifties refuse to talk about their experiences at the school to this day.

I never attended a funeral at the school except my own, and that was during a dream. Was that a sign of my impending fate? If my mother hadn't contacted the school, would I be here to tell my story? That happened more than sixty two years ago, and I still wonder about that dream, and my life.

⸻ ❧ ⸻

As I began to write my memoir, unexplained events and situations have surfaced. After this conversation with Nate, I was haunted for weeks with "what if." What if we buried guys who were murdered as a result of the "underground assignment," or the captured runaways, or the boys who were beat to death in the Ice Cream Factory? I remembered the holes we were told to dig. Did they only bury dead animals in those holes? Animals did die at the plantation. I do remember burying them and filling in the graves, but I don't remember that many animals dying.

We dug a lot of holes and sometimes we were ordered to fill in holes that had been dug by the guys who worked on the alternate days. I was young and didn't give it much thought at that time. We were given orders and we followed them blindly. Now, as a man looking back to that time, a lot of unanswered questions and loose ends have caused me to wonder. Did the State of Florida consider the animals to be more valuable than us slaves?

Upon reviewing the Erin Kimmerle report of the investigation of the Dozier school, one report that stuck with me referred to the recording of deaths and burial sites of deceased boys. That report stated that Dozier was the only facility (reform school, penal institution, hospital, or the like) throughout the nation that was unable to account for missing or deceased residents. When I think about the unaccountable amount of missing or presumed dead boys, there would be no organized cemetery if their bodies needed to be hidden.

We, the younger boys, dug holes all around the edges of the 1400 acre grounds. We never actually knew why there were those times when a hole or graves was partially filled with just enough dirt to cover whatever was buried there, and we never gave it a second thought. Did some person(s) place a dead boy in the hole under the darkness of night and leave it for the slave boys to complete the burial during the day?

There were always four boys working a burial hole. Why wasn't the grave completely covered by the team working the site before the end of a workday? Why were boys told to dig a hole in the afternoon, knowing there wouldn't be enough time to complete the burial before the end of the workday, and then the even day/odd day crew would have to complete the job the next day?

I wonder, did the secret assassins of Dozier, the corrupt staff, need an open grave to hide their crime? The question is, who or what team placed the animal or human in the hole and partially covered it? When we were told to bury a dead animal, we dug the hole earlier in the workday, the tractor was used to put the animal in the hole, and the grave was covered. Now, after my conversation with Nate, I wonder if I buried one or more of my murdered brothers.

Were the twenty eight sets of remains discovered in April 2019 really those of only animals? What about the other undiscovered remains scattered over the property? I know there are other graves because we dug the holes.

This is Cottage is believed to be Lee Cottage, the last quarters where I was housed before departing from the Florida School for Boys in 1959. All the cottages were very similar to each other. This picture was taken in 2016. This is the side where Black boys lived. Credited to Richard Huntly.

CHAPTER 25
Return to the Town
of Marianna

A candlelight vigil was held on the Jackson County Courthouse steps despite a warning not to hold this event. 2012 was a busy year for the Black Boys at Dozier Reform School. That was also the year we resigned our membership from the White House Boys. We were asked by their president not to return to Marianna to hold a candlelight vigil under any circumstances without permission, or we would be disowned by the WHB organization.

We formed The Black Boys at Dozier Reform School group at that point. We continued to make arrangements for a first time ever program in recognition of our lost and dead brothers by having that candlelight vigil in their honor. We were invited by the former mayor and sheriff to select any location we wanted. We chose the courthouse steps in Mariana, Florida. At the time, we didn't know the history of what took place in that general location except that it was in the town where the reform school was located. However, eighty-one years earlier, a Black man named Mr. Claude Neal was hung on a large branch overlooking the same courthouse steps.

One of the town ladies pulled me to the side and said we were the first Black men they ever let speak from that position in their town. Maybe I could say we held a candlelight vigil for our wrongfully hung brother Mr. Claude Neal at the same time.

The day of the candlelight vigil was a busy one for me and other members of Black Boys at Dozier. I can't say this event was so important to me. As I walked and talked to people they seemed to be quite open and friendly; it was hard to believe some of the things I heard about Jackson County. I am always cautious not to get too comfortable in strange settings, especially after learning the history of a bad location.

That day in 2012, people were moving about like it was a gathering, a get together. I felt a tugging on my shirt as I spoke to people here and there. I looked around and a soft spoken older lady, much older than she looked, asked to speak with me.

"I want to talk with you about something," she said.

"Okay," I told her. "I'd like to hear it," listening for her every word. "What is it you want to tell me?" I asked.

Softly, she began to speak. "There are so many things I could tell you. It's been a long time now. We're all tired of holding stuff in. It's not right. It jest ain't right. Jest about everybody in this town knows the history of what happened here, but they're scared to talk. After all these years, some of them are still scared."

I stood listening to her carefully.

She continued. "Some of these houses you see round hea' right now still got jars on their fireplaces with meat in 'dem, right now! Canning jars they call 'em."

My interest was at its peak. I wanted to know what she was talking about that she just had to tell me.

She went on. "In those jars is alcohol with meat in 'em. A certain part of the Black man in 'em; ya know what I mean? It is a lot more stuff I want to tell y'all. I have a lot of friends that know what happened here was wrong. They are scared to talk. Me and my friends got a lot we can tell y'all, but like I said, they are scared."

I told her, "If you all want to talk with me, we can find a private spot to meet. I will come to you and get your story. In about three weeks we'll be back for our last conference. If I see you at the conference, I'll know you are still ready to talk with me."

Three weeks later, we returned to the grounds of Dozier to do our last press conference for 2012. The lady and her friends were going to meet me at the conference, but no one showed up. I didn't question their motives. I never spoke with her again.

In August of 2013, on the north side of the campus, The Black Boys at Dozier, gave a press release. Through the media, the world was shocked to hear about Florida's best kept secret of hiding the bodies of boys as young as six years old in unmarked graves. These young boys had no name, no face, and no records of their existence. They were committed in a place unknown to the world, and alone. I guess the masters of the plantation didn't know that eventually there would be no hiding of the boys who were buried in secret.

The book of Revelation, chapter 20, verse 13, reads as follows: "And the sea gave up the dead which were in it; and death and hell delivered up the dead which were in them: and they were judged every man according to their works."

The names of the people in this chapter have been withheld for the safety of all involved and for various reasons by request.

CHAPTER 26
Looking Back

A few years after I left the Florida School for Boys, I realized I was struggling to turn my life around. The only thing I remembered was that I didn't remember learning any job-related skills while being detained. My understanding was clear. The time spent working those long hard winter and summer days, I did learn a valuable lesson: I learned to survive, and survival gave me a future. With survival came dedication to myself, and to hell with Jim Crow, White Cap, Alexander, Dozier, Mitchell, Mobley, and etc. They labeled me "incorrigible" and I will own it with pride.

Being incorrigible didn't allow me to bend my back to be subservient. The Reverend Doctor Martin Luther King, Jr. once said, "Whenever men and women straighten their backs up, they are going somewhere, because a man can't ride your back unless it is bent." I have and will always have scars; they will always be with me, but I took my incorrigible self and turned it into a good life. Mrs. Hawkins taught me a good life began with an education.

I traveled the country, settling in Alabama, married, had children, and served in the US Army, stationed at Ft. Lewis near Tacoma, Washington during the Viet Nam era. I had life experience, but I always remembered how much

I wanted that education. A formal education would allow me to further straighten my back. I enrolled in Chattanooga Valley Community College in Phenix City, AL. where I earned my GED with the help of my two oldest daughters, Sabrina and Regina.

In addition to earning my high school diploma, it was through the Lord's grace that I studies and learned the basic principles of business and entrepreneurship. I worked for Combine Insurance Company, where I was one of their accident insurance salesmen in Alabama. After returning to Florida, I successfully owned several businesses, from a tree removal service to real estate investing.

My life after Dozier was nothing short of amazing. Hostility and anger had almost devoured me, but staying true to who I was took me from the plain name "Huntly" to Mr. Huntly, and from driving in a Mercury to driving a Mercedes. The Lord had plans for me and all that praying paid off. He has also allowed me to write and share my story so my past will never be forgotten. I am retired, a proud father, grandfather, great grandfather, and great great grandfather. I've lived a fruitful life, and I am happy and content. I am blessed. ***I survived.***

PART 4
DOZIER
IN PICTURES

Following are some of the pictures from the Florida School for Boys aka Arthur G. Dozier School for Boys.

Photos are credited to Florida Memory Archives in Tallahassee, Florida unless otherwise indicated.

Typical school day at the library for the colored students in the 1950's and 60's. About 30 encyclopedias. No teacher.

Typical school day for the Whites, 1940s to 60s.

We were called colored boys and they call this separate but equal opportunity in the 1940's to 60's. Poor working conditions and no teachers.

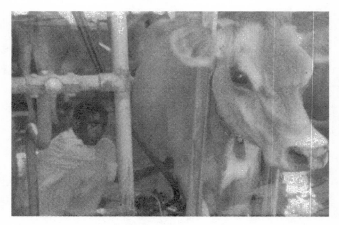

Twelve-year old milking a cow before daybreak.

I was only eleven years old when I was taken to the White House and Beaten. I died that day in 1957. A pain no man can explain.

Warehouse manager training. A certificate job, ready for tomorrow. This was available for White students only.

Plumbing classes. These guys would leave the school with a plumbing certificate.

Machine shop classes. They will also receive a certificate and ready for the world.

Watching the same show, different time, same place. Blacks are separated from Whites; no benches for Black boys to sit on. (Contrast with the picture below)

Happy times. Whites going on a fun trip for the day in the 1950s.

Hard times. Black boys going to work the fields in the 1950s.

Scooping chicken poop, feeding them and gathering eggs. This was a White boy's job.

Tending the hog farm. Eleven and twelve year old boys ran the farm like grown men. This is a Black Boy's job

Black boys loading hay in the fields until they are drop-dead tired.

Left to right, Arthur G. Dozier, Governor Claud Kirk, and Mitchell, superintendent of the Black side when I was there in 1957 to '59.

THE YELLOW JACKET   Saturday, December 28, 1957

Cottage Father W. J. Mobley and a group of colored boys from Ft. Lauderdale are pictured while on a shopping trip to Marianna, where, through the generosity of Judge Dorr S. Davis of that city, the students each had $2.00 to spend for gifts.

1957 picture of Mobley and boys

Boot Hill Cemetery. North side campus about seventy-five yards behind Lee Cottage. 55 bodies were unearthed

here. 55 balloons were released. Florida School for
Boys aka Arthur G. Dozier School for Boys opened in
Jan. 1900. Credited to: R. Huntly, April 6th, 2018.